NEW YORK

In brief

New York is a vibrant, larger-than-life cosmopolitan city with unflagging energy and a competitive streak whether on Wall Street or in the arts. It grew up vertically on a handful of islands watched over by the Statue of Liberty, amid noise and frenzied activity, ever intent on doing things bigger and faster. Manhattan stretches from the East River to the Hudson, a checkerboard of narrow glass canyons and shady streets of townhouses. It has many faces: sophisticated along Fifth Avenue, bohemian and intellectual in Greenwich Village, bustling on Times Square and Broadway, bucolic in Central Park, artistic in Chelsea, trendsetting in TriBeCa, SoHo and NoLIta. Visitors have an infinite choice of things to do: museums, music, art galleries, theater – Broadway and off. The borough of Brooklyn, Manhattan's sprawling neighbor, is no less fascinating, with its diverse, lively 'villages' (DUMBO, Williamsburg, Cobble Hill), a mix of elegant brownstones, lofts and warehouses taken over by artists and writers. Further on, the melting pot of Queens is home to Greeks, Chinese, Hispanics and many more. The city is dotted with neighborhood cafés, lounge bars, diners, restaurants serving food from all over the globe, flea markets, boutiques, jazz clubs, arts venues... All these, and more, are now within your reach thanks to this MapGuide.

Find your bearings in New York

A Downtown / TriBeCa
B SoHo / Greenwich Village / Meatpacking / Chelsea
C Chinatown / NoLIta / Lower East Side / East Village
D Times Square / Theater District / Rockefeller Center
E Midtown East / Fifth Avenue
F Upper West Side
G Upper East Side
H Central Park / Harlem
I Brooklyn Heights / DUMBO / BoCoCa / Park Slope
J Williamsburg / Queens

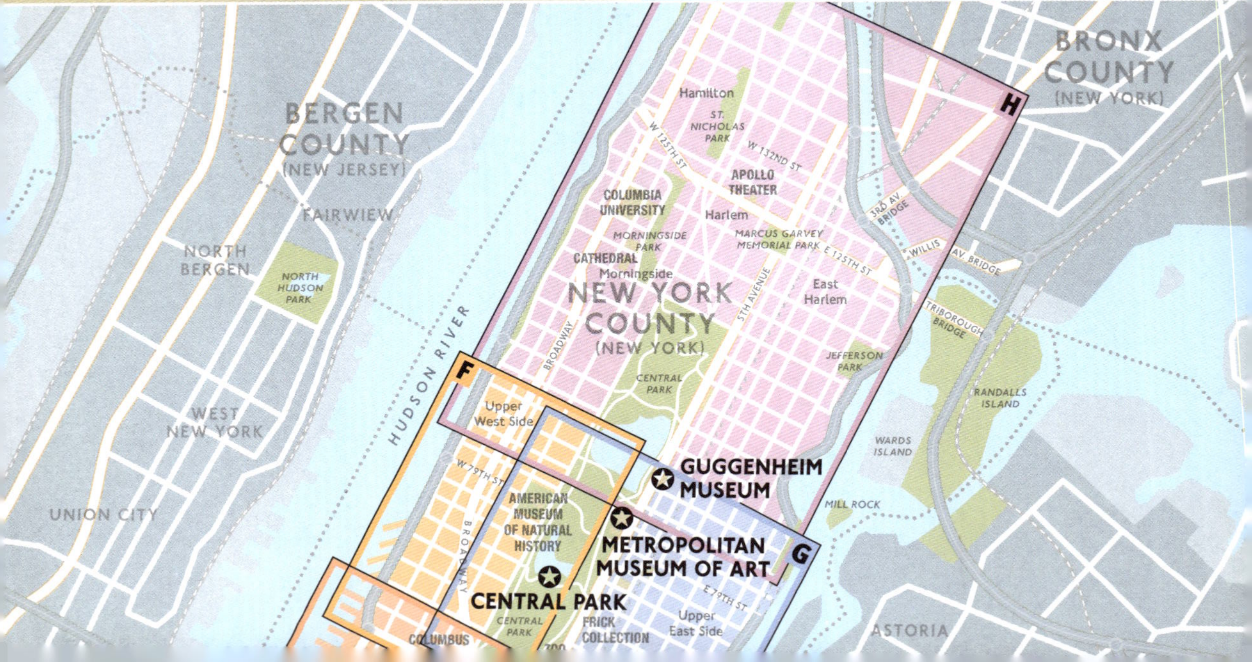

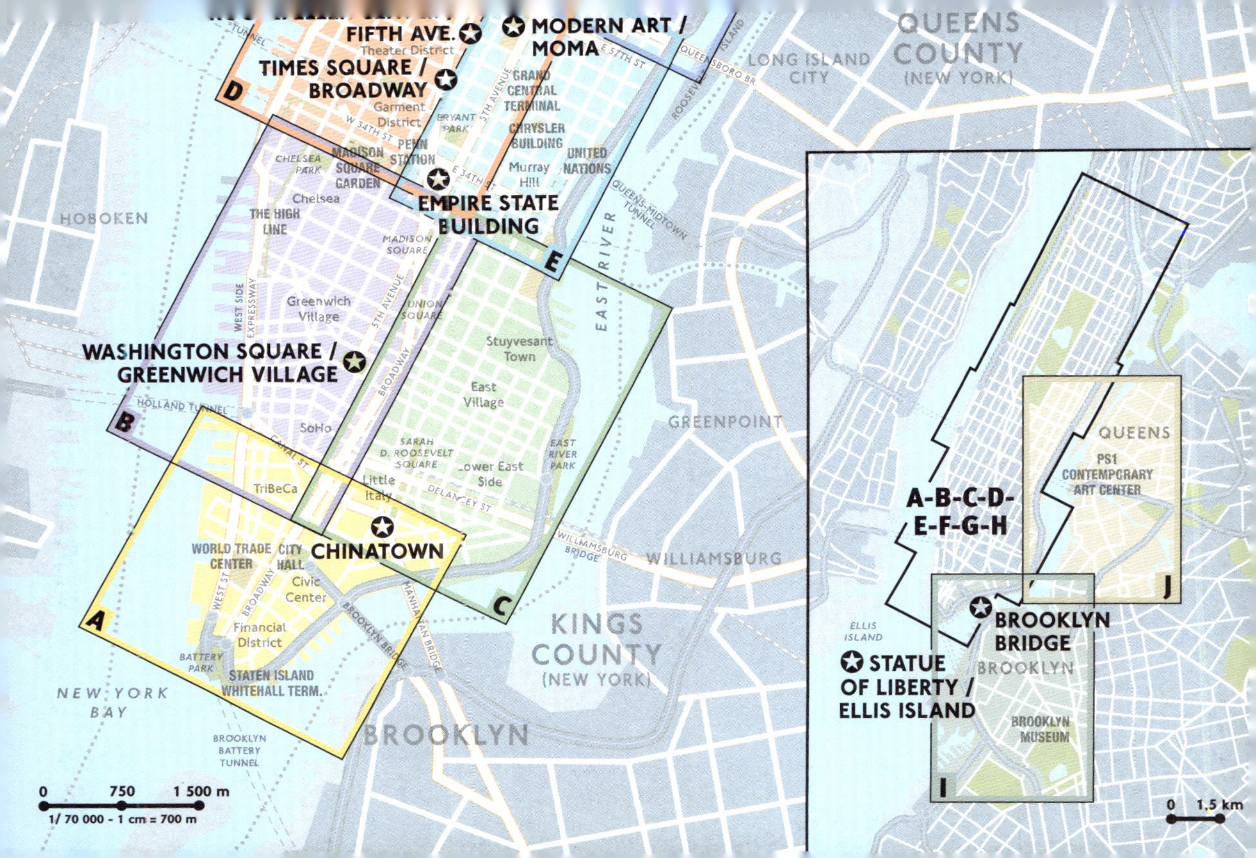
FIFTH AVE.
MODERN ART / MOMA
Theater District
TIMES SQUARE / BROADWAY
Garment District
BRYANT PARK
5TH AVENUE
GRAND CENTRAL TERMINAL
CHRYSLER BUILDING
UNITED NATIONS
Murray Hill
W 34TH ST
PENN STATION
MADISON SQUARE GARDEN
CHELSEA PARK
E 34TH ST
E 57TH ST
EMPIRE STATE BUILDING
Chelsea
THE HIGH LINE
MADISON SQUARE
HOBOKEN
WEST SIDE EXPRESSWAY
Greenwich Village
UNION SQUARE
BROADWAY
Stuyvesant Town
East Village
WASHINGTON SQUARE / GREENWICH VILLAGE
HOLLAND TUNNEL
SoHo
CANAL ST
SARAH D. ROOSEVELT SQUARE
Lower East Side
EAST RIVER PARK
EAST RIVER
Little Italy
DELANCEY ST
TriBeCa
CHINATOWN
WORLD TRADE CENTER
CITY HALL
Civic Center
WEST ST
Financial District
BATTERY PARK
STATEN ISLAND WHITEHALL TERM.
BROOKLYN BRIDGE
MANHATTAN BRIDGE
WILLIAMSBURG BRIDGE
WILLIAMSBURG
GREENPOINT
QUEENS-MIDTOWN TUNNEL
QUEENSBORO BR.
ROOSEVELT ISLAND
LONG ISLAND CITY
QUEENS COUNTY (NEW YORK)
KINGS COUNTY (NEW YORK)
NEW YORK BAY
BROOKLYN BATTERY TUNNEL
BROOKLYN
TUNNEL
A
B
C
D
E
0 750 1 500 m
1/ 70 000 - 1 cm = 700 m
A-B-C-D-E-F-G-H
QUEENS
PS1 CONTEMPORARY ART CENTER
J
ELLIS ISLAND
STATUE OF LIBERTY / ELLIS ISLAND
BROOKLYN BRIDGE
BROOKLYN
BROOKLYN MUSEUM
I
0 1,5 km

9/11 MEMORIAL

→ *July 4*
Fireworks display over the East River.
Mostly Mozart Festival
→ *End July-end Aug*
Concerts and shows at Lincoln Center (**F** B5).
Summer Streets
→ *First three Saturdays in Aug (7am–1pm)*
7 miles of pedestrian-only streets in the middle of Manhattan: walks, races, games, music.
Tennis US Open
→ *End Aug-mid Sep*
In Flushing Meadows (Queens).
Restaurant Week
→ *Two weeks or more during July-Aug*
See January-February.
September
Labor Day weekend
→ *Weekend prior to the first Mon in Sep (public holiday)*
Caribbean Carnival in Brooklyn.
Feast of St Gennaro
→ *Ten days mid Sep*
Celebrations all around Little Italy.
October
Columbus Day
→ *Second Mon of the month*
Parade along Fifth Avenue.
Halloween Parade
→ *Oct 31*
Parade on Sixth Avenue, starting from West Village.
November
New York Marathon
→ *One Sun in early Nov*
Staten Island to Central Park, via the five boroughs.
Thanksgiving Day
→ *Last Thu of the month*
Huge parade on Broadway, between Central Park and Macy's.
December
Christmas lights
→ *The whole month*
Don't miss the Rockefeller Center Christmas tree (**D** E2).
New Year's Eve
Ball drop countdown in Times Square (**D** E3); fireworks in Central Park.

MONEY MATTERS

State taxes
A state and city tax of 8.875 percent is added to restaurant food and most music, clothing and electronic goods. Clothing and footwear less than $110 are tax free.
Discounts in museums
Discounts are available to students and those over 60; they vary depending on the museum.
Free entry to museums
Museums' entrance fees are often high so here are a few tips:
Pay-What-You-Wish
→ *Suggested donation at Museo del Barrio, Brooklyn Museum, MoMA PS1, Cloisters, American Museum of Natural History, the Museum of the City of New York and others.*
Free entry or Pay-What-You-Wish
→ *Brooklyn Botanic Garden:*

ARCHITECTURE

Federal style (1780–1830)
Introduction of English neoclassical style; City Hall interiors (**A** D2).
Greek Revival style (1820–50): Inspired by Greek architecture; Federal Hall (**A** D3).
Gothic Revival (1840–80): Inspired by European Gothic style (end of 12th–15th c.); Trinity Church (**A** C3).
Italianate and Second Empire (1880–1900): Mixture of Haussmann and Italian Renaissance styles; **brownstones** (made of rich brown sandstone); **Washington Square Row** (**B** C4).
Beaux-Arts (1890–1920): Mixture of neo-Baroque and classical styles; **Public Library** (**E** A3); **Little Singer Building** (**B** D5).
Skyscrapers (20th–21st century):
The Chicago School designed the first skyscrapers at the end of the 19th century. They have since been built in a variety of styles: Gothic – **Woolworth Building** (**A** C2); neo Renaissance – **Flatiron Building** (**B** D1); Art Deco – **Chrysler Building** (**E** B4); International – **United Nations** (**E** D3); Post-modern – 432 Park Ave by Rafael Viñoly (**E** B1); 220 Central Park South by Robert A. M. Stern (**F** D6); Late Modern – **NY Times Building** (**D** D3), **New York** by Frank Gehry (**A** D2), **1 WTC** (**A** C2) by Skidmore, Owings and Merrill.

CITY PROFILE

- Five boroughs: Manhattan, Brooklyn, Bronx, Queens and Staten Island
- Spread over three islands: **Manhattan, Staten Island** and part of **Long Island** (the boroughs of Brooklyn and Queens). The Bronx is the only borough built on the mainland itself
- The city is separated from New Jersey by the Hudson River
- 8.5 million inhabitants, of whom 1.6 million live in Manhattan
- 60.3 million visitors in 2016

NEW YORK BOROUGHS

WWW.

→ *nycgo.com*
Official website of the NYC tourism organization.
→ *nyc-architecture.com*
New York's most famous buildings; plus themed walking tours.
→ *timeout.com/newyork*
Cultural events listing.

TOURIST INFO

Official NYC Information Center (D E4)
→ *Macy's Herald Square, 151 W 34th St (Broadway) Tel. (212) 484 1222 Daily 9am (Sat 10am, Sun 11am)–7pm*
See website for other locations (*nycgo.com*).

Brooklyn Tourism & Visitor Center (I B3)
→ *Brooklyn Borough Hall, 209 Joralemon St (Court) Tel. (718) 802 3700 Mon-Fri 10am–6pm nycgo.com/brooklyn*

NYC Information Center (A E3)
→ *South Street Seaport, Horn Blower Cruises, Pier 15; Daily 9am–7pm (5pm Sep-April)*

TELEPHONE

212, 917 and 646 are the area codes for Manhattan; 718 and 929 are the codes for New York's four other boroughs; 347 is the code for part of Manhattan as well as the outer boroughs.

To call NY from abroad
→ *00 + 1 (USA) + area code + the seven-digit number*

To call abroad from NY
→ *Dial 011 + country code + area code + local number*

Emergency numbers
Police, fire brigade
→ *Tel. 911*

Useful numbers
Directory enquiries (national)
→ *Tel. 1 + area code + 555 1212*

Collect calls
→ *Tel. 1-800-COLLECT*

Lost and Found
→ *Tel. 511*
For subway and bus lost property.

DIARY OF EVENTS

Public holidays
→ *New Year's Day; Martin Luther King Jr Day (third Mon in Jan); Presidents Day (third Mon in Feb); Memorial Day (last Mon in May); Independence Day (July 4); Labor Day (first Mon in Sep); Columbus Day (second Mon in Oct); Veterans Day (Nov 11); Thanksgiving (fourth Thu in Nov); Christmas Day*

January-February

Martin Luther King Jr Day
→ *Third Mon in Jan*
To mark the birthday of the civil rights activist; there is also a parade along Fifth Ave at the end of Jan.

Restaurant Week
→ *One or more weekend Feb-beg March*
Cheaper prix-fixe menus in high-end restaurants.

Chinese New Year Festival
→ *Jan or Feb (varies)*
Carnival and fireworks in Chinatown.

March-April

St Patrick's Day
→ *March 17*
Parade along Fifth Avenue.

Armory Show
→ *Half a week in March*
Contemporary art fair at Piers 92, 94 (**D** B1).

Easter Parade
→ *Easter Sunday*
Procession along Fifth Avenue.

TriBeCa Film Festival
→ *10 days, mid-late April*
International film festival.

May-June

Memorial Day
→ *Last Mon in May*

Shakespeare in the Park
→ *Usually June-Aug*
Free theater in Central Park

July-August

Independence Day

Top ten

Sights of New York you should not miss

✪ Statue of Liberty/ Ellis Island (**A** A4)
This iconic symbol of both New York and America, representing Liberty lighting up the world, was a gift from France to commemorate the 100th anniversary of the United States. On a small island, at the entrance to the harbor, it is right beside Ellis Island, which once acted as a gateway for millions of immigrants, at an average rate of 5,000 per day. It marked the entry to a new world promising hope for a better future.

✪ Washington Square/Greenwich Village (**B** C4)
Washington Square is the city's downtown bohemian meeting place, attracting artists, students, musicians and chess players around its fountain. Many of the surrounding buildings belong to New York University. Close by, Greenwich Village, with its jazz clubs, bars, fashionable boutiques and shady streets, offers a welcome relief from the frenetic pace elsewhere, and the chance to explore the haunts of beat poets from the past.

✪ Chinatown (**C** A6)
One of New York's most chaotic neighborhoods, it represents a microcosm of China crammed into a few blocks. Here you'll find stalls selling cheap pirated goods, kitsch bazaars, markets with exotic vegetables, herbalists and old men playing mah jong in the parks.

✪ Times Square/ Broadway (**D** E3)
Times Square is the city's nerve center: raucous, hectic and irresistible, with its huge billboards, multicolored neons and motley selection of stores, all set off by a kaleidoscopic array of flashing lights at night. Tourists from all over the world flock to the wealth of theaters on Broadway, where outsize posters trumpet the latest plays and musicals as a constant stream of yellow taxis pours by.

✪ Rockefeller Center (**D** E2)**/Fifth Avenue** (**E** A1-A6)
The 13 Art Deco buildings of Rockefeller Center, the city's first large complex, are organized around its famous flag-draped plaza. Just below, an enormous golden Prometheus plays host to a skating rink or attractive terrace, depending on the season. The highest building offers a breathtaking view of Central Park. From here, it is just a short walk to Fifth Avenue.

✪ Modern art in the MoMA (**D** F1) **and the Guggenheim Museum** (**G** C1)
The Museum of Modern Art is arguably the finest museum of its kind in the world, with a dazzling parade of masterpieces (Monet, Matisse, Picasso, Hopper, Warhol, etc.). The treasure trail continues in the Guggenheim Museum, a prodigious spiraled building designed by Frank Lloyd Wright.

✪ Empire State Building (**E** A5)
Ever since its construction in 1931, this tower has provided the best vantage point for an aerial view of the city. Its inimitable outline, crowned with a thin antenna, was immortalized in 1933, when King Kong placed his captive blonde on its summit. Its terrace, the setting for countless romantic scenes (Cary Grant and Deborah Kerr in the 1957 movie *An Affair to Remember*, for example) offers a stunning view of the jungle of skyscrapers below.

✪ Central Park (**G** B2)
This expanse of green in the midst of the skyscrapers is an improbable luxury in a city relentlessly devoured by real estate. Central Park unfurls a procession of ponds, wooded hills, secret paths, rolling lawns and esplanades dating back a hundred years. A place to jog, row, skate, read, cycle, stroll, dream...

✪ Metropolitan Museum of Art (**G** C1)
The Met provides a wondrous journey through 5,000 years of art and history from all the continents. European masters of painting and sculpture from the Middle Ages to the 19th century, American art, Pre-Colombian treasures, totems from the Pacific, Greek and Roman statues and 15 Islamic galleries including a medieval Maghrebi-Andalusian tiled courtyard. The collections are so extensive that they cannot possibly be absorbed in a single day.

✪ Brooklyn Bridge (**I** B1)
This bridge, built in 1870–83 over the East River, connects Lower Manhattan with Brooklyn. The imposing forms of its two gray stone pylons have made it one of New York's most striking symbols. A stroll along the pedestrian walkway, early in the morning or at dusk, reveals matchless views of the skyscrapers in the Financial District and the boats going in and out of the harbor.

CENTRAL PARK

ROCKEFELLER CENTER

TIMES SQUARE

MOMA

VIEW OF MANHATTAN FROM THE EMPIRE STATE BUILDING

WALL STREET

TRINITY CHURCH

WORLD TRADE CENTER / 9/11 M

★ Ellis Island Immigration Museum (A4)
→ *Tel. (212) 363 3200*
Ferry from Battery Park
Daily 9.30am–5pm
(extended hours in summer)
More than 12 million immigrants in search of a better life entered the United States through a French Renaissance Revival building on Ellis Island, now a museum with exhibits.

★ Statue of Liberty (A4)
→ *Details as above*
Reservations are necessary to enter the crown of this 151-ft-high gift from France to the United States in 1886. 'Liberty Enlightening the World' was designed by Auguste Bartholdi with an interior support structure by Gustave Eiffel. Shipped in pieces from France, it was built on Bedloe's Island in New York Harbor, where it has stood for over a century, a symbol of freedom.

★ Battery Park / Hudson River Walk (C4)
This is the former site of 17th-century gun batteries, now a public garden with views of Staten Island and the Statue of Liberty. At its center is Castle Clinton, built in 1811 to defend the island of Manhattan against the British. Take the walk north along the Hudson.

★ World Trade Center (C3)
→ *Church / Vesey / West / Liberty Sts*
This site includes 1 WTC by David Childs; Bjarke Ingel's Tower 2; Richard Rogers' Tower 3; Fumihiko Maki's Tower 4 and Santiago Calatrava's soaring Transportation Hub, Oculus. Childs', Maki's and Calatrava's are the only ones open. See the 9/11 Memorial of two pools with waterfalls and oak trees in the footprints of the original Twin Towers (free pass at 20 Vesey St or online).

9/11 Memorial Museum
→ *180 Greenwich St; Tel. (2*
266 5211; Daily 9am–8pm
(9pm Fri-Sat, 7pm in winter)
911memorial.org/museum
A dark, almost 11,000 sq. ft. space 70 feet below ground is a haunting retelling of the facts of th day: photographs, artifac (from the 60-ft-high 'slur wall to a fire truck or a watch) recordings of final phone calls, videos, and an unseen space with unidentified remains.

★ Museum of Jewish Heritage (B4)
→ *36 Battery Place*
Tel. (646) 437 4202

STATUE OF LIBERTY

ELLIS ISLAND IMMIGRATION MUSEUM

BATTERY PARK

A Downtown / TriBeCa

At the southern tip of Manhattan the old warehouses of Fulton Street and South Street Seaport stand in contrast to today's Wall Street and Hudson Yards skyscrapers. In the evening, traders desert downtown and the financial frenzy of the day abates. This is the perfect time for a stroll along the South Street Seaport, or for a boat ride to the Statue of Liberty. To the north, TriBeCa (Triangle below Canal Street), with its former industrial buildings, is a hub for the downtown art, food and shopping scenes.

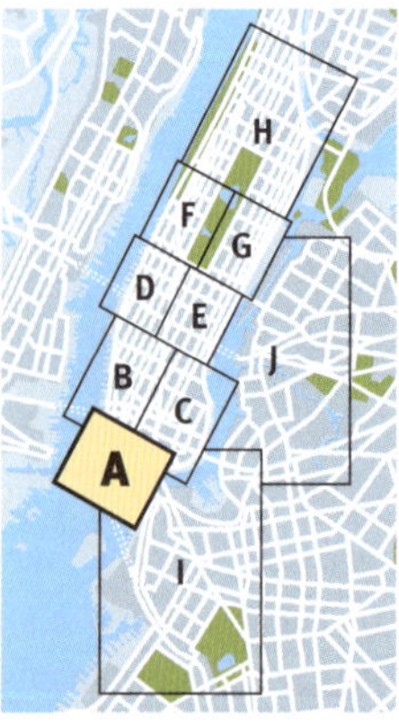

ADRIENNE'S PIZZA BAR

LOCANDA VERDE

RESTAURANTS

Mission Chinese (F1) 🍴1
→ *171 East Broadway (Rutgers); Tel. (212) 529 8800; Mon-Fri 5.30pm–midnight (11pm Mon); Sat-Sun noon–4pm, 5.30pm–midnight (11pm Sun)*
Sink into a red leather booth and experience Danny Bowien's spicy California Sichuan cooking. Entrées $9–40.

Hudson Eats (B2) 🍴2
→ *Brookfield Pl, 230 Vesey St; Mon-Sat 7am (10am Sat)–9pm; Sun 11am–7pm*
Among the 20 restaurants to try are: Dig Inn, Amada, Blue Ribbon Sushi, Dos Toros, Mighty Quinn's, Northern Tiger and the vast French marketplace, Le District, with a wine bar, patisserie, espresso bar, gourmet stations for sandwiches or a smoked duck salad; three formal restaurants and an outdoor space on the water. Entrées $10–29.

North End Grill (B2) 🍴3
→ *104 North End Ave (Murray)*
Tel. (646) 747 1600
Mon-Fri 11.30am–10pm (10.30pm Fri); Sat-Sun 11am–10.30pm (9pm Sun)
This Danny Meyer outpost serves up lunch, dinner and brunch (on weekends) with an imaginative, appealing menu. Entrées $28–59.

Blaue Gans (C2) 🍴4
→ *139 Duane St (Church and W Broadway)*
Tel. (212) 571 8880
Mon-Sat 11am–midnight
Vintage film, art posters and a zinc bar set the tone in this bistro with delicious Austro-German fare. Entrées $19–32.

Adrienne's Pizza Bar (D3) 🍴5
→ *54 Stone St (Hanover Sq.) Tel. (212) 248 3838; Daily 11am–midnight (10pm Sun)*
This small, lively spot is popular for its pizza and salads, wine choices and outdoor dining in summer. Pizza $17–24.

Locanda Verde (B1) 🍴6
→ *377 Greenwich St (North Moore); Tel. (212) 925 3797; Daily 7am (8am Sat-Sun)–3pm, 5.30–11pm (11.30pm Fri-Sat)*
Robert De Niro is a partner in this Italian taverna with a working fireplace and a kitchen helmed by chef Andrew Carmellini. Entrées $25–39.

The Odeon (C1) 🍴7
→ *145 W Broadway (Duane and Thomas)*

ANE PARK PATISSERIE

BRANDY LIBRARY

KORIN

Tel. (212) 233 0507
Daily 8am (10am Sat-Sun)–midnight (11pm Sun-Tue)
This legendary spot is a neighborhood and art world favorite. Classic brasserie menu. Entrées $17–40.

Augustine (D2) 8
→ 5 Beekman St (Nassau)
Tel. 212 375 0010; Daily 7.30am (10am Sat-Sun)–3.30pm, 5.30–11pm (10pm Sun; midnight Fri-Sat)
Signature Keith McNally in a French bistro with light dishes and the classics, including grill and rotisserie. Great brunch. Entrees $26–36.

PATISSERIE, CAFÉS, BARS

Edward's (C1) 9
→ 136 W Broadway (Duane and Thomas); Tel. (212) 233 6436; Daily 9am–midnight (dinner from 5pm)
Have a drink at the bar of this cozy bistro. Sidewalk seating in summer.

Smith & Mills (B1) 10
→ 71 N Moore St (Greenwich)
Tel. (212) 226 2515; Daily 11am–2am (3am Thu-Sat)
In a former carriage house, 'Heritage' style vintage marble, padded banquettes and yellowing maps on the walls. Large selection of drinks, salads, entrées.

La Colombe Coffee (C1) 11
→ 319 Church St (Lispenard)
Tel. (212) 343 1515
Daily 7.30am (8.30am Sat-Sun)–6.30pm
Have great coffee from Philadelphia with cookies or croissants in the morning, or tartines from City Bakery in the afternoon.

Weather Up (C1) 12
→ 159 Duane St (Hudson)
Tel. (212) 766 3202
Mon-Sat 5pm–midnight (2am Thu-Sat, 11pm Sun)
Dim lighting, with white subway tiles, this sleek bar has a cool vibe and interesting drinks and bites. Also at 589 Vanderbilt Avenue (I D4).

Brandy Library (C1) 13
→ 25 N Moore St (Varick)
Tel. (212) 226 5545
Sun-Wed 5pm–1am; Thu-Sat 4pm–2am (4am Fri-Sat)
This cozy bar serves brandy and cocktails, with a great menu.

Blacktail (C4) 14
→ 22 Battery Place, Pier A Harbor House; Tel. (212) 785 0153; Daily 5pm–2am
This bar evokes Prohibition-era Havana with its dark wood walls, vintage art, highballs, and sours; steaks to veggie rice and beans.

Duane Park Patisserie (B2) 15
→ 179 Duane St (Greenwich)
Tel. (212) 274 8447; Daily 8am–7pm (5pm Sun)
Owner and pastry chef Madeline creates amazing peanut butter cookies and molten chocolate cake.

The Bennett (C1) 16
→ 134 W Broadway
Mon-Fri 5pm–2am (1am Mon-Wed); Sat-Sun 11am–2am (11pm Sun)
Stylish and cheerful with blue velvet banquettes, imaginative cocktails and a delicious brunch and dinner menu.

SHOPPING

Korin (C2) 17
→ 57 Warren St (W Broadway); Tel. (212) 587 7021; Daily 10am–7pm (6pm Sat-Sun)
The best in Japanese and western knives as well as Japanese tableware.

Nili Lotan (B2) 18
→ 188 Duane St (Greenwich and Hudson)
Tel. (212) 219 8794
Daily noon–7pm (6pm Sun)
Minimalist women's clothes in mostly white, black and midnight blue.

Steven Alan (B1) 19
→ 103 Franklin St (Church and W Broadway)
Tel. (212) 343 0692
Mon-Sat 11.30am–7pm (8pm Thu); Sun noon–6pm
Young, hip men's, women's and children's clothing and accessories.

Westfield World Trade Center (C2) 20
→ 185 Greenwich St
Tel. (212) 284 9982; Mon-Sat 10am–9pm; Sun 11am–7pm; hours of restaurants and stores may vary
Inside Santiago Calatrava's soaring subway station, Oculus, this three-level mall has an Apple store, Eataly, Lacoste, MAC, Shake Shack and Victoria's Secret.

Century 21 (C3) 21
→ 22 Cortlandt St (Broadway); Tel. (212) 227 9092; Mon-Fri 7.45am–9pm (9.30pm Thu-Fri); Sat 10am–9pm; Sun 11am–8pm
Haute-couture at discount prices: Versace, Ralph Lauren, Prada and Calvin Klein at 40–70 percent discount.

Brookfield Place (B2) 22
→ 230 Vesey St
Among the 40 shops in this mall are: Tory Burch, J. Crew, DVF, Theory, Club Monaco, Hermès, Burberry, Bottega Veneta, Ferragamo, Vince and Vilebrequin.

NATIONAL MUSEUM OF THE AMERICAN INDIAN

MUSEUM OF JEWISH HERITAGE

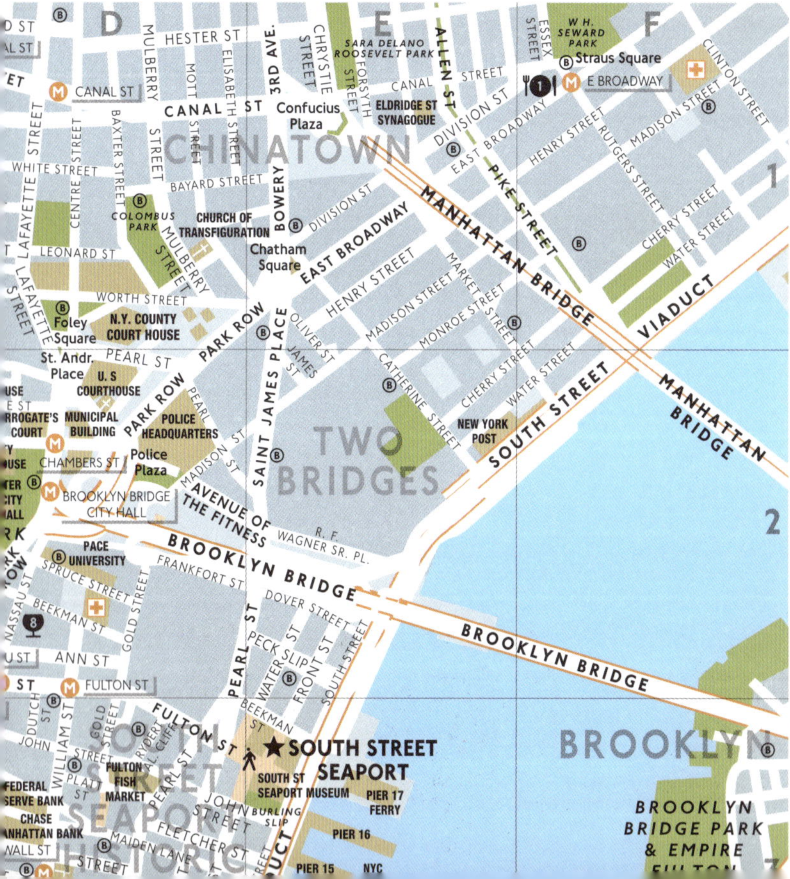

WOOLWORTH BUILDING

SOUTH STREET SEAPORT

n-Fri 10am–5.45pm
pm Wed, 5pm Fri)
's memorial to the
locaust displays
wish art and traditions
the 19th century, a
rospective of the rise
Nazism and a tribute to
wish-American artists;
nporary exhibitions.

National Museum the American dian (C4)
1 Bowling Green
(212) 514 3700
ily 10am–5pm (8pm Thu)
the US Customs House ce 1994, it is at the base Broadway, originally an cient Indian footpath t ran almost all the way up to what is now Boston. Native American historical exhibitions and Native American contemporary artists.

★ **Wall Street** (D3)
The narrowness of the street accentuates the extraordinary height of the skyscrapers. At 8–18 Broad St, behind the façade of the New York Stock Exchange, watch the frenetic transactions of the New York floor traders.

★ **Trinity Church** (C3)
→ *Broadway (West Wall)*
Tel. (212) 602 0800
Daily 7am–6pm
In its day, this Gothic Revival-style building, with its 280-ft spire, was the tallest monument in the city and a landmark for passing ships. In the shade of the 100-year-old oak trees in the cemetery rest celebrated members of Colonial America.

★ **Woolworth Building** (C2)
→ *233 Broadway (Barclay)*
Five-and-dime store king Frank Woolworth commissioned this building in 1910. Three years later the tallest building in the city opened: an enormous 57-story Gothic structure with marble walls and Byzantine -style mosaic ceilings – all exalting the virtues of work and prosperity.

★ **South Street Seaport** (E3)
→ *12 Fulton St*
Brownstones and cobble stone streets preserve the vestiges of the city's port in the 19th century. There are galleries, restaurants, boutiques; the new Pier 17 mall has shops, fine restaurants, and a rooftop terrace for events.

South Street Seaport Museum (E3)
→ *12 Fulton St; Tel. (212) 748 8600; Wed-Sun 11am–5pm*
A fleet of historic ships and exhibitions on New York's maritime past.

RUBIN MUSEUM OF ART

WHITNEY MUSEUM

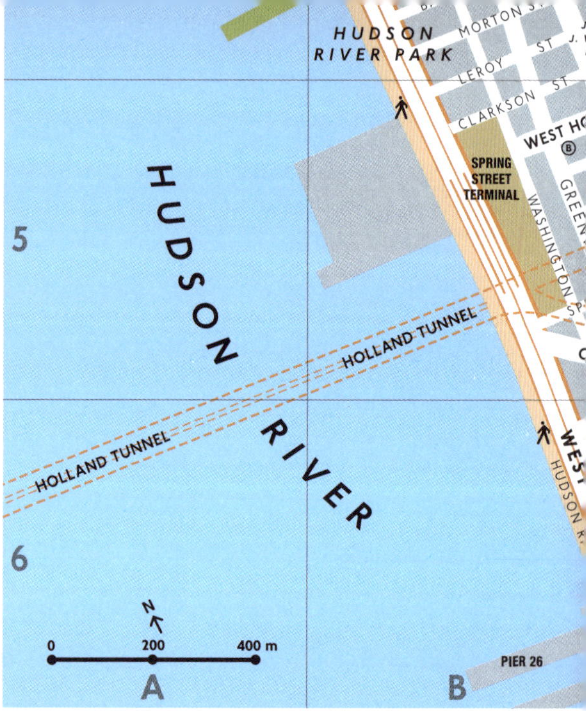

◀ Map A

★ Center for Architecture (D4)
→ *536 La Guardia Place Tel. (212) 683 0023; Mon-Fri 9am–8pm; Sat 11am–5pm*
This 1911 building was converted to house the AIA New York Chapter, which was founded in 1857. Exhibitions on design, planning and architecture.

★ SoHo Historic District (D5)
→ *Between Canal and Houston Sts, from W Broadway to Lafayette St*
Twenty blocks of elegant 19th-century brownstones: Greene (nos 28–30 and 72–76), Prince (cross street Broadway), as well as the length of Broadway (cross street Broome). Italian colonnades, Victorian cornices and plenty of Beaux-Arts-style windows characterize the façades of these buildings. Artist Donald Judd's building is at 101 Spring St.

★ Washington Square (C4)
→ *Washington Square*
A meeting place for street performers, chess players, folk musicians and students. At the north end, Washington Centennial Memorial Arch (1892) commemorates the 100th anniversary of George Washington's presidential inauguration. The north end has some of the city's best examples of Greek Revival architecture. Henry James (1882–1916), Edward Hopper (1882–1967) and John Dos Passos (1896–1970) lived here.

★ Rubin Museum of Art (C2)
→ *150 W 17th St (Seventh) Tel. (212) 620 5000 Wed-Mon 11am–5pm (9pm Wed, 10pm Fri, 6pm Sat-Sun)*
A small, elegant museum devoted to the art of the Himalayas and surrounding regions: sculpture, textiles, paintings and objects from the 2nd to the 20th centuries. Great shows and lectures.

★ The High Line (A3)
→ *Gansevoort to 34th Sts Daily 7am–7pm (Apr-May, Oct-Nov 10pm, June-Sep 11p*
Inspired by the Promena Plantée in Paris, Field Operations and Diller Scofidio & Renfro have turned Gansevoort to 34t streets – a 1.45-mile two-story high freight train track – into a public spac designed by Piet Puldolf. You can walk through the former Cudahy meatpacking plant buildings and, in the fina section, along the tracks without trees, there is a lawn and wildflower

SOHO HISTORIC DISTRICT

CENTER FOR ARCHITECTURE

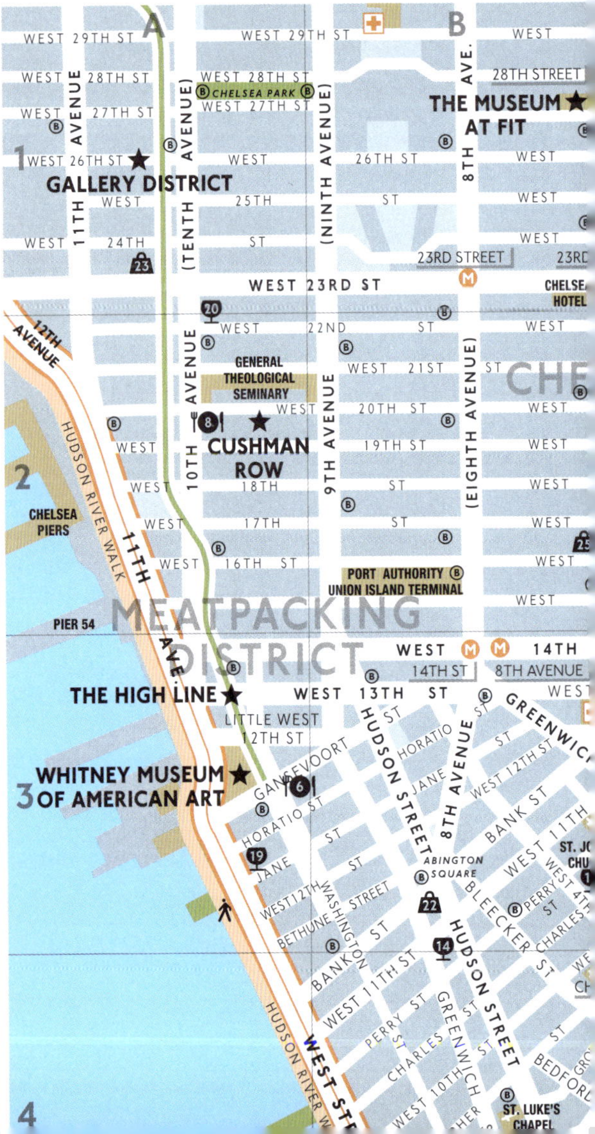

Stretching north and west from Broadway and Canal Street all the way up to West 30th Street and the Hudson River are SoHo, Greenwich Village, the Meatpacking District and Chelsea. Soho's former industrial buildings are filled with fashionable shops, museums, galleries and restaurants. Greenwich Village is buzzing with stores and jazz clubs; the Meatpacking District has turned its buildings into bars and boutiques, and Chelsea is filled with art galleries, clubs and eateries.

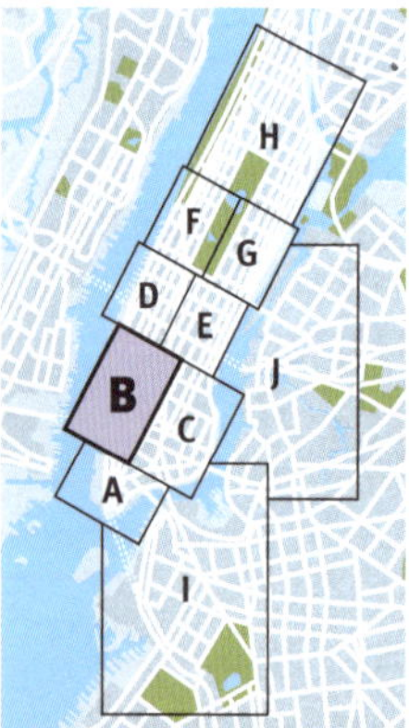

MISS LILY'S

COOKSHOP

RESTAURANTS

Paowalla (C5) 1
→ *195 Spring St (Sullivan) Tel. (212) 235 1098; Daily noon (11.30am Sat-Sun)–2.30pm, 5.30–11pm*
Floyd Cardoz, formerly of Tabla, offers a Goan menu. Entrees $13–32.

Le Coucou (D6) 2
→ *138 Lafayette St (Howard); Tel. (212) 271 4252; Daily 7am–2pm, 5–11pm (10pm Sun)*
Daniel Rose's nod to French classics in an elegant space; breakfast, brunch and dinner. Entrees $24–48.

Via Carota (B4) 3
→ *51 Grove St (Seventh Ave South); Tel. (212) 255 1962 Daily 11am–midnight*
A trattoria serving perfect Italian food. Entrées $16–20. Also try their I Sodi restaurant on 105 Christopher St (B4).

Miss Lily's (C4) 4
→ *132 W Houston St (Sullivan)*
Tel. (212) 812 1482; Daily 11.30am–5pm, 6–11.30pm (12.30am Thu-Sat)
Island cuisine and Caribbean music played by a DJ. Entrées $18–28. Another Miss Lily's at 109 Avenue (E 7th St).

Indochine (D4) 5
→ *430 Lafayette St (Fourth) Tel. (212) 505 5111 Daily 5.30pm–midnight (11pm Sun-Wed)*
A scene with beautiful staff serving delicious Vietnamese food. Entrées $22–33.

Santina (A3) 6
→ *820 Washington St (Gansevoort); Tel. (212) 254 3000; Daily 10am–midnight*
A glass box under the Highline, with Venetian chandeliers and a delicious 'coastal Italian' menu. Entrées $16–39.

Cosme (D2) 7
→ *35 East 21st St (Park Ave) Tel. (212) 913 9659; Daily noon (11.30am Sat-Sun)–2.30pm, 5.30–11pm (midnight Fri-Sat)*
Star chef Enrique Olvera serves up Mexican dishes brilliantly tweaked. $13–35. Atla on Lafayette St is also by Olvera.

Cookshop (A2) 8
→ *156 Tenth Ave (20th) Tel. (212) 924 4440 Daily 8am (10am Sat-Sun)–11.30pm*
Lively, with an open kitchen: duck, trout, fried rabbit; outdoor seating. Entrées $19–48.

abcV (D2) 9
→ *38 E 19th St (Broadway) Tel. (212) 475 5829; Mon-Fri 8am–10.30am, noon–3pm, 5.30–10.30pm (11pm Thu-Fri); Sat 5.30–11.30pm*

AGNOLIA BAKERY

VILLAGE VANGUARD

ABC CARPET & HOME

Jean-Georges serves only non-GMO, plant-based, organic, farm produce. $9–18.

CAFÉS, TEAROOMS

City Bakery (C2) 10
→ *3 W 18th St (Fifth)*
Tel. (212) 366 1414
Mon-Fri 7.30am–6pm; Sat 8am–6pm; Sun 9am–6pm
Cookies and salads from the Union Square Greenmarket.

Buvette (B4) 11
→ *42 Grove St (Bleecker)*
Tel. (212) 255 3590
Daily 7am–2am
Charming bistro for breakfast, lunch and dinner; delicious madeleines, croque monsieurs and tartines.

Eataly (C1) 12
→ *200 Fifth Ave (23rd)*
Tel. (212) 229 2560
Daily 9am–11pm
With 14 places to eat, this market sells pasta, prosciuttos, cheese and more. La Birreria beer garden is on the rooftop.

Ladurée (D5) 13
→ *398 W Broadway (Spring and Broome)*
Tel. (646) 392 7868
Daily 8am (9am Sat-Sun) –9pm (10pm Fri-Sat)
Have tea, breakfast, lunch or dinner; also an outdoor terrace, macaron and pastry shop.

Magnolia Bakery (B3) 14
→ *401 Bleecker St (11th)*
Tel. (212) 462 2572
Daily 9.30am–11pm (midnight Fri-Sat)
New Yorkers line up to buy these cupcakes.

BARS, CLUBS, CONCERTS

Balthazar (D5) 15
→ *80 Spring St (Crosby)*
Tel. (212) 965 1414
Mon-Fri 7.30am–midnight (1am Fri); Sat-Sun 8am–1am (midnight Sun)
Keith McNally's brasserie has a vast bar for scene-watching.

Jimmy (C5) 16
→ *15 Thompson St (Grand)*
Tel. (212) 201 9118; Daily 5pm–1am (2am Thu-Sat)
On the 18th floor of the James Hotel: great views, a fireplace and an outdoor pool on a teak deck.

Village Vanguard (B3) 17
→ *178 Seventh Ave South (Perry and 11th)*
Tel. (212) 255 4037
Sets: 8.30pm, 10.30pm daily
For over 60 years the best names have played here. Cover charge $30.

Blue Note (C4) 18
→ *131 W 3rd St (MacDougal)*
Tel. (212) 475 8592
Concerts daily 8pm, 10.30pm (also 12.30am Fri-Sat); Sun brunch at 11.30am, 1.30pm
A legendary address in the jazz world, with world-class artists.

The Jane Hotel Ballroom (A3) 19
→ *113 Jane St (West)*
Tel. (212) 924 6700
A vast fireplace, stuffed trophies, and leather and velvet couches add to the old-world atmosphere.

Empire Diner (A2) 20
→ *210 10th Ave (22nd St)*
Tel. (212) 335 2277
Daily 5pm–1am
Fun for drinks and small plates.

SHOPPING

All the following shops are open daily

Greenwich Village (B3-D4) 21
Marc by Marc Jacobs
→ *403 Bleecker St*
Lulu Guinness
→ *394 Bleecker St*
Screaming Mimi's
→ *382 Lafayette St*

Meatpacking District (B3) 22
→ *14th St and Abingdon Sq.*
Chic shopping, eating and living in this former meat market neighborhood.
Jeffrey
→ *449 W 14th St (Tenth)*
Vince
→ *833 Washington St (W 12th)*

Chelsea galleries (A1-2) 23
Hauser & Wirth (*511 W 18th St*), **Zwirner** (*519, 525 and 533 W 19th St, 537 W 20th St*), **Matthew Marks Gallery** (*523 W 24th St, 502, 522 and 526 W 22nd St*), **Gagosian Gallery** (*555 W 24th St and 522 W 21st St*), **Paula Cooper Gallery** (*534 and 521 W 21st St*).

SoHo (D5) 24
→ *Between Grand, Prince, Thompson and Lafayette Sts*
Galleries and boutiques.
Uniqlo
→ *546 Broadway (Spring); flagship at 666 Fifth Ave*
Alexander Wang
→ *103 Grand St*
Prada
→ *575 Broadway (Prince)*

ABC Carpet & Home (D2) 25
→ *888 Broadway (E 19th)*
Tel. (212) 473 3000
Mon-Sat 10am–7pm (8pm Thu); Sun 11am–6.30pm
China, glassware, pillows, toys, jewelry and furniture.

Barney's (C2) 25
→ *101 7th Ave; Tel. (646) 264 6400; Daily 10am (11am Sun)–7pm (8pm Thu)*
Five floors of men's and women's clothing; and Fred's restaurant.

THE HIGH LINE

CUSHMAN ROW

▶ Map E

▼ Map C

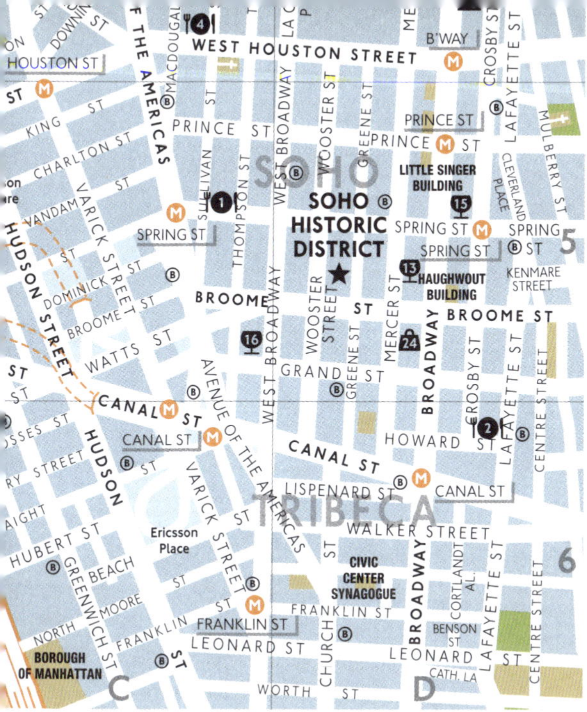

MADISON SQUARE PARK

THE MUSEUM AT FIT

◀ Map A

ld. The best time to go
early morning or sunset.

Cushman Row (A2)
406 418 W 20th St
e of the best examples
Greek Revival
whouses. The exteriors
te from 1840 (cornicing,
le windows on the attic
or decorated with laurel
lands), all characteristic
owhouses – identical,
active red-brick houses.

Gallery strict (A1)
Between 21st and 29th (10th and 11th)
-June: Tue-Sat 11am–6pm
350 plus art
leries located in former
rehouses are the places
to see contemporary art. Thursday is opening night and the streets are festive.

★ Flatiron Building (D1)
→ *175 Fifth Ave; Open to visitors during office hours*
Erected in 1902 to house the Fuller Construction Company, this was the first skyscraper in New York. It resembles a flatiron, but its triangular shape is due to the layout of Broadway. The first four floors are clad with limestone and Italian Renaissance motifs; terracotta is used for the upper stories. Until 1909 it was the tallest building in the world (285 ft).

★ The Museum at FIT (B1)
→ *Seventh Ave (27th); Tue-Fri noon–8pm; Sat 10am–5pm*
Attached to the prestigious Fashion Institute of Technology, where Calvin Klein and other famous American designers were trained, this museum presents excellent exhibitions on themes around fashion, muses and designers.

★ Whitney Museum of American Art (A3)
→ *99 Gansevoort St (Washington St); Wed-Mon 10.30am–6pm (10pm Fri-Sat)*
Designed by Renzo Piano, the 220,000 square feet encompass a theater on the 3rd floor, a permanent collection on the 6th and 7th, temporary shows on the 8th, as well as Danny Meyer's Studio Café; his restaurant, Untitled, is on ground level.

★ Madison Square Park (D1)
→ *23rd St (Fifth)*
A beautiful, lush park with a great view of the Empire State Building to the north and the Flatiron to the south. Crowds line up at the Shake Shack in the middle of the park for its famous burgers, reputed to be amongst the best in the city.

THE MUSEUM AT ELDRIDGE ST

LOWER EAST SIDE TENEMENT MUSEUM

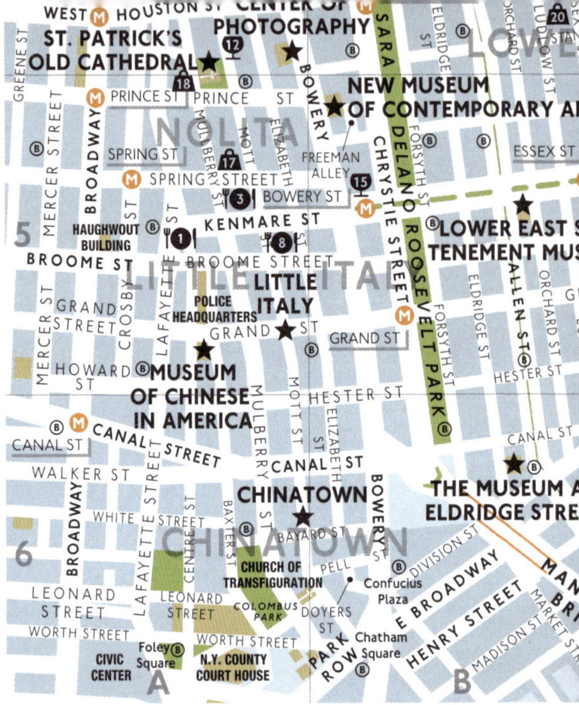

★ **Chinatown** (A6)
→ *Around Confucius Plaza (Bowery and Division)*
Pagoda-shaped roofs, Buddhist temples, stalls, restaurants with their signs in Chinese... this is a very lively area during Chinese New Year.

★ **The Museum at Eldridge Street** (B6)
→ *12 Eldridge St*
Tel. (212) 219 0302
Sun-Fri 10am–5pm (3pm Fri); guided tour of synagogue and museum every hour (last tour 4pm)
This first Eastern European Ashkenazic synagogue in America was built in 1887 by Russian and Polish Jewish immigrants. The interior has beautiful carved wood balconies and magnificent chandeliers. A small museum traces the history of the Jewish community in Manhattan.

★ **Little Italy** (A5)
Mulberry Street was the stronghold of the New York-Italian community before it moved to the Bronx and Brooklyn. Today, busy trattorias and pizzerias mostly cater to tourists.

★ **Museum of Chinese in America (MOCA)** (A5)
→ *211-215 Centre St (Grand); Tel. (855) 955 6622*
Tue-Sun 11am–6pm (9pm Thu)
In this musuem, the history of Chinese immigration in Manhattan is traced through artifacts, photos and audio tapes.

★ **Lower East Side Tenement Museum** (B5)
→ *103 Orchard St*
Tel. (877) 975 3786
Guided tours only: daily 10am–6pm (last tour 5pm)
These small, plain tenement buildings were once home to immigrant families living in the most deplorable conditions. Guided tours of the restored apartments offer insights into the life of an Irish couple in 1869, or an Italian Catholic family during the Depression.

★ **St Mark's Place** (B3
Tompkins Square, which welcomed the sit-in protesters in the sixties, marks the starting point this long street lined wit trees and brownstones. At the junction of Second Avenue and 10th St is St Mark's Church-in-the-Bowery. On this site ther was once a chapel which marked the boundaries the Bowery farm belongi to Peter Stuyvesant, last governor of the colony o New Amsterdam. The current church, a sober elegant neoclassical-sty construction, was erecte

◀ Map A

MUSEUM OF CHINESE IN AMERICA

CHINATOWN

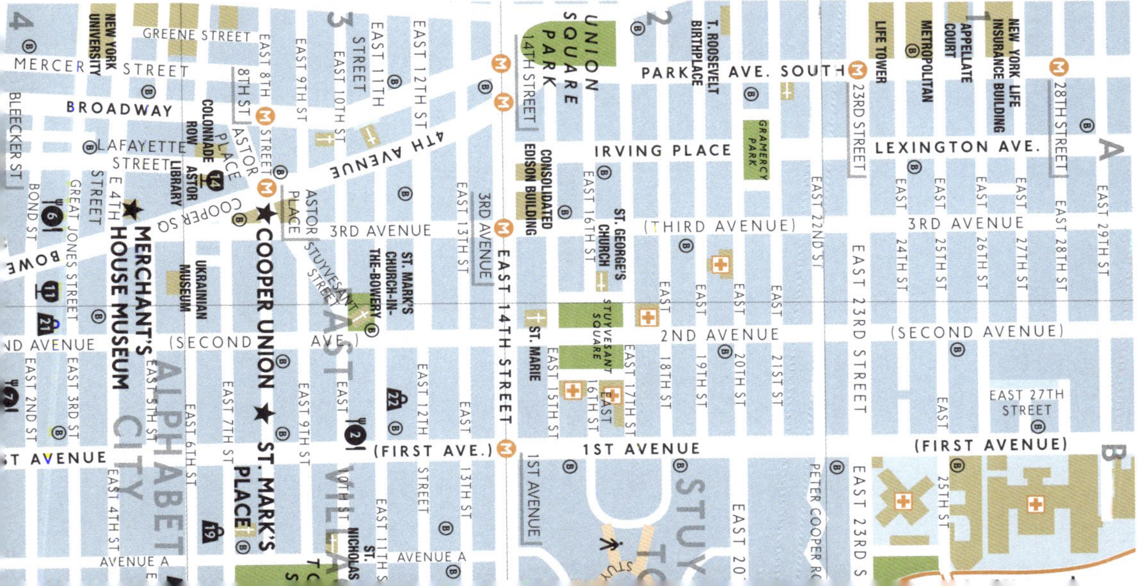

Destination of successive waves of immigrants, this area stretches north from Fulton and Franklin Streets, with Chinese, Italian and Central European communities eager to express their culture and traditions. Chinatown, Little Italy, Lower East Side... you can take a world tour minutes from the corporate skyscrapers of Wall Street. Further north, in the East Village, hub of the Beat Generation of the 1950s, and now the millennials, are many fashionable bars and restaurants.

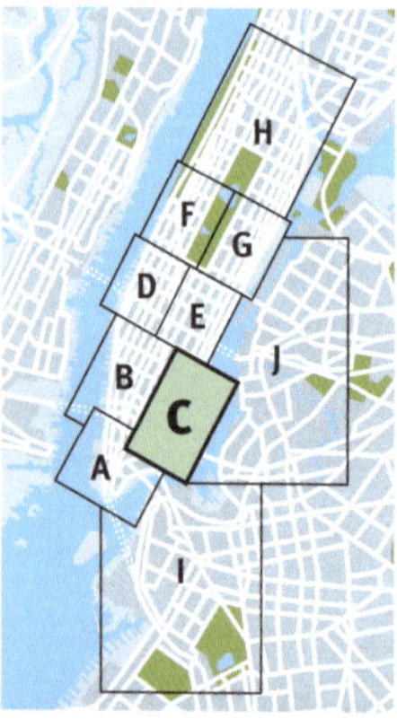

MOMOFUKU NOODLE BAR

KATZ'S DELI

RESTAURANTS

La Esquina (A5) 🍴1
→ *114 Kenmare St (Lafayette)*
Tel. (646) 613 7100
Daily 11am–2am
A fake taco-stand front has a door that leads to the basement restaurant for delicious Mexican food. Entrées $6–37. A small outpost with counters and one table at 200 W 55th St (**D** E1).

Momofuku Noodle Bar (B3) 🍴2
→ *171 First Ave; Tel. (212) 777 7773; Daily noon–4.30pm (4pm Sat-Sun), 5.30–11pm (1am Fri-Sat)*
Star chef David Chang's noodle bar. Don't miss his famous BBQ pork buns and fried rice cakes. Six other spots: Ssäm Bar, Ko, Milk Bar, Má Pêche, Booker and Dax, Nishi. Entrées $12–18. No reservations.

Pasquale Jones (A5) 🍴3
→ *187 Mulberry St (Kenmare); Daily 5.30–11pm (10pm Sun); lunch Fri-Sun noon–3pm*
Italian food and small plates, with creative wood-fired pizzas in an elegant, modern space. Entrées $21–65.

Ivan Ramen (C4) 🍴4
→ *25 Clinton St (Stanton)*
Tel. (646) 678 3859
Daily noon–3.30pm, 5.30pm–midnight
A storefront space with two counters and two small dining areas: try the spicy red chili ramen and triple pork, triple garlic *mazemen*. Entrées $15–16.

Katz's Deli (B4) 🍴5
→ *205 E Houston St (Ludlow)*
Tel. (212) 254 2246; Mon-Fri 8am–10.45pm (2.45am Thu, midnight Fri); Sat open 24hrs; Sun noon–10.45pm
One of New York's most famous delis, opened in 1888. $4–30.

Il Buco Alimentari & Vineria (A4) 🍴6
→ *53 Great Jones St (Bowery and Lafayette)*
Tel. (212) 837 2622
Daily 7am (11am Sat-Sun)–11pm (midnight Fri-Sat).
A rustic bakery, food shop and trattoria. Entrées $19–34. Try the original Il Buco at 47 Bond St (Bowery).

Prune (B4) 🍴7
→ *54 E First St (First and Second Ave)*
Tel. (212) 677 6221; Daily 5.30–11pm (also 10am–3.30pm Sat-Sun)
Chef Gabrielle Hamilton's tiny restaurant serves fantastic brunch and dinner; brunch is worth the wait. Entrées $16–33.

WERY BALLROOM

MANHATTAN PORTAGE

A-1 RECORDS

De Maria (A5) 8
→ *19 Kenmare St (Elizabeth and Bowery) Tel. (212) 966 3058; Daily 8.30am (9am Sat-Sun)–10pm (11pm Sat-Sun)*
In a modern space, healthy breakfast, lunch, and dinner, as well as inventive, herbal juices and cocktails; try the grain bowls and striped bass. Entrees $14–24.

TEAROOM, ICE-CREAM PARLOR

sugar Sweet sunshine (C5) 9
→ *126 Rivington St (Norfolk) Tel. (212) 995 1960; Mon-Fri 8am–10pm (11pm Fri); Sat-Sun 10am–11pm (Sun 7pm)*
Great variety of cupcakes, cakes and cookies.

Il Laboratorio del Gelato (B4) 10
→ *188 Ludlow St (Houston) Tel. (212) 343 9922 Mon-Fri 7.30am–10pm (midnight Fri); Sat-Sun 10am–10pm (midnight Sat)*
Excellent artisanal gelati, not too sweet, in flavors that change seasonally.

BARS, CONCERTS

Lobby Bar (A4) 11
Bowery Hotel, 335 Bowery Tel. (212) 505 9100; Daily 5pm–4am (2am Sun-Wed)
Cozy, lively retro space with a fire going in the winter; for summer, try the patio upstairs.

DBGB (A4) 12
→ *299 Bowery (Houston) Tel. (212) 933 5300 Mon-Thu 5pm–midnight (11pm Mon); Fri-Sun noon (11am Sat-Sun)–3pm, 5pm–1am (11pm Sun)*
A modern space from Daniel Boulud with a great bar where you can order off the main menu.

Schiller's Liquor Bar (C5) 13
→ *131 Rivington St (Norfolk) Tel. (212) 260 4555 Mon-Wed noon–midnight; Thu-Fri noon–1am; Sat-Sun 10am–1am (midnight Sun)*
Keith McNally's nod to a French working-class restaurant with a bar and wine served in carafes marked Cheap, Decent, Good. Entrées $13–21.

Joe's Pub (A3) 14
→ *425 Lafayette St (Astor Place); Tel. (212) 539 8500 Daily 6pm–1am*
A quirky supper club with live performances by actors, writers and musicians.

Bowery Ballroom (B5) 15
6 Delancey St (Bowery) Tel. (212) 533 2111 Daily from 8pm
A large music venue with a varied program: world music, rock, pop, etc; bar area in the basement.

Nuyorican Poets Cafe (C4) 16
→ *236 E Third St (Ave C) Tel. (212) 780 9386; hours vary according to program*
A bastion of the Nuyorican (New York + Puertorican) art movement of the 1970s; theater, poetry, slam (Fri 10pm), hip-hop, jazz, salsa and more.

SHOPPING

Shopping in NoLIta (A5) 17
→ *Between Mulberry, Houston, Elizabeth and Kenmare Sts; the shops below are open daily (Sun from 11am or noon)*
NoLIta stands for North of Little Italy: the area has many stores, bars and restaurants.

Sigerson Morrison
→ *28 Prince St (Mott) Tel. (212) 219 3893*
Stylish, pricey shoes.

Tory Sport
→ *257 Elizabeth St (Prince and E Houston) Tel. (212) 334 3000*
Well-priced, stylish clothing for women.

Manhattan Portage
→ *258 Elizabeth St Tel. (212) 226 9655*
More than 100 styles of strap-on bags and totes.

McNally Jackson Books (A5) 18
→ *52 Prince St (Mulberry and Lafayette) Tel. (212) 274 1160; Daily 10am–10pm (Sun 9pm)*
A well-curated bookstore; also has magazines. Café.

A-1 Records (B3) 19
→ *439 E 6th St (Ave A) Tel. (212) 473 2870 Daily 1-9pm*
From rare to newly released, vinyl records cover genres as varied as jazz and hip hop.

Reformation (B4) 20
→ *156 Ludlow St (Stanton) Tel. (646) 448 4925 Daily noon–8pm (7pm Sun)*
Hip, eco-conscious, USA-made, inexpensive women's clothing.
Also at 23 Howard Street (**B** D6).

John Derian (B4) 21
→ *6-10 E Second St (Second Ave and Bowery); Tel. (212) 677 3917; Tue-Sun 11am–7pm*
Three small shops packed with linens, china, furniture, art by Hugo Guinness, and much more.

Xenomonia (B3) 22
→ *206 E Sixth St Tel. (646) 590 3211 Tue-Fri noon–7pm*
Textiles, rugs, jewelry and furniture from India, Iran and Uzbekistan.

NEW MUSEUM
OF CONTEMPORARY ART

ST PATRICK'S
OLD CATHEDRAL

MERCHANT'S HOUSE MUSEUM

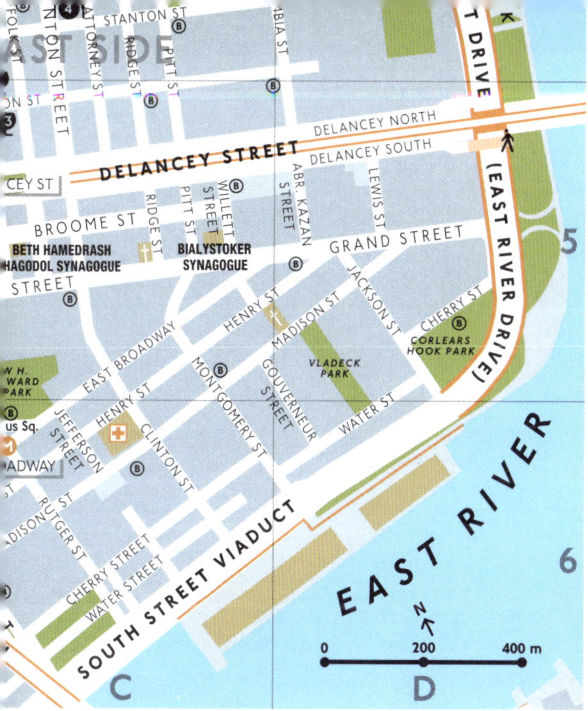

ST MARK'S PLACE

COOPER UNION

1799, in the heart of
tle Ukraine. Its Greek
vival steeple was added
1828 and the Italianate
rtico in 1858.

New Museum of
ntemporary Art (B5)
235 Bowery (Stanton
d Rivington)
(212) 219 1222; Tue-Sun
m–6pm (9pm Thu)
zuyo Sejima and Ryue
hizawa of the Tokyo
n SANNA designed this
ven-story, 60,000-sq.-ft
ace clad in opaque zinc-
ated steel, made up
three main gallery
ors, a 182-seat theater
he basement and a
nthouse. Contemporary
exhibitions.

★ St Patrick's Old Cathedral (A4)
→ *263 Mulberry St*
Tel. (212) 226 8075
Daily 8am–6pm (8pm Sun)
This is the second oldest Catholic church in the city. From 1809 to 1879 it served as New York's Archdiocese church, up until the construction of St Patrick's Cathedral on Fifth Avenue. Its austere façade hides a Gothic Revival interior.

★ Merchant's House Museum (A4)
→ *29 E Fourth St*
Tel. (212) 777 1089
Thu-Mon noon–5pm (8pm Thu)
Built in 1832 for the rich merchant Seabury Tredwell, this Greek Revival-style rowhouse became a museum in 1936. The original furniture and layout has been retained, proviving a reflection on the lives of the upper classes in 19th-century New York.

★ Cooper Union (A3)
→ *41 Cooper Square (Astor Place); no visits*
Peter Cooper, millionnaire and philanthropist, wished for a co-education school of art and techniques that would be open to all, regardless of class, sex or racial background. It opened in 1859 in a superb Italianate brownstone building. Today it is one of the oldest steel-beamed buildings still standing.

★ International Center of Photography (A4)
→ *250 Bowery (Prince)*
Tel. (212) 857 0003
Tue-Sun 10am–6pm
The Gwathmey Siegel space has two floors and three galleries for exhibitions; their vast archive of over 60,000 photographs includes the work of Henri Cartier-Bresson, Robert Capa, Eve Arnold, Weegee, Dorothea Lange, and even images of Oppenheimer and the Bomb. Café and bookstore.

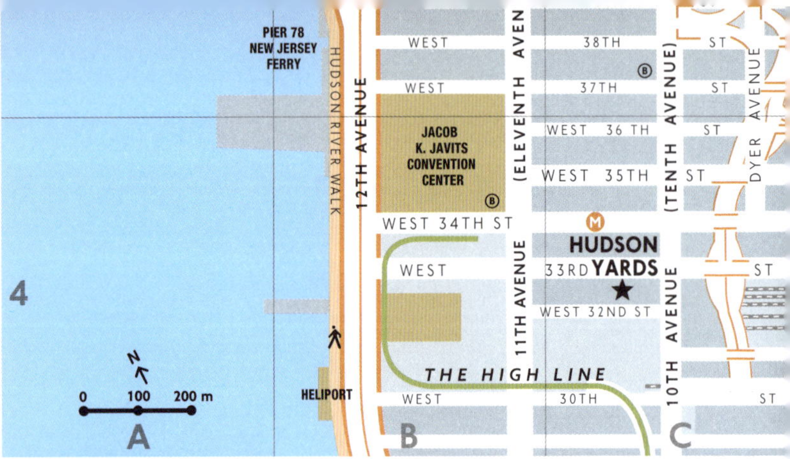

INTRECID SEA, AIR AND SPACE MUSEUM

ROCKEFELLER CENTER

TOP OF THE ROCK

★ General Post Office (D4)
→ *Eighth Ave (31st and 33rd)*
Tel. (212) 330 3296
Mon-Fri 7am–10pm; Sat 9am–9pm; Sun 11am–7pm
There is still talk of converting a portion of the building into a new concourse of Amtrak (but not until 2020). This huge 1933 McKim, Mead & White building is inspired by a neoclassical temple.

★ Bryant Park (E3)
→ *Sixth Ave (42nd)*
This formally planted oasis behind the main branch of the New York Public Library shows classic films in the summer. Get a snack from Tom Colicchio's 'wichcraft outlet, in an outdoor kiosk.

★ Times Square (E3)
→ *Broadway (Seventh)*
Surrounded by state-of-the-art illuminated billboards, Times Square is a hub of activity. The nerve center of the Theater District, it is best seen at night when the huge video screens are lit.

★ Madame Tussauds (D3)
→ *234 W 42nd St (Seventh and Eighth)*
Tel. (866) 841 3505; Daily 10am–8pm (10pm Fri-Sat)
Angelina Jolie, Brad Pitt, Fidel Castro and Bob Dylan are among the realistic wax figures of over 200 of the world's top celebrities set in themed areas with interactive exhibits; check out the gift shop.

★ Rockefeller Center (E2)
→ *Rockefeller Plaza (49th)*
This is one of the world's first commercial complexes (1931–39) designed by the leading light of the American Art Deco movement, architect Raymond Hood. The 19 buildings within the complex are arranged in a gridiron pattern, laid out around the famous Rockefeller Plaza.

Rockefeller Plaza (F2)
→ *W 49th St / W 50th St*
From Fifth Avenue, the Channel Gardens lead to the lower plaza, an ice rin in winter, overlooked by a gilded bronze statue of Prometheus by Paul Manship. At Christmas ar enormous 130-ft Christma tree is placed behind it.

Top of the Rock (E2)
→ *Daily 8am–midnight*
From the GE Building (no. 30) are stunning vie of the city from the Top o the Rock observatory.

Radio City Music Hall (E2)
→ *1260 Sixth Ave (50th)*
Tel. (866) 858 0007 for sho / (212) 247 4777 for guided

GENERAL POST OFFICE

BRYANT PARK

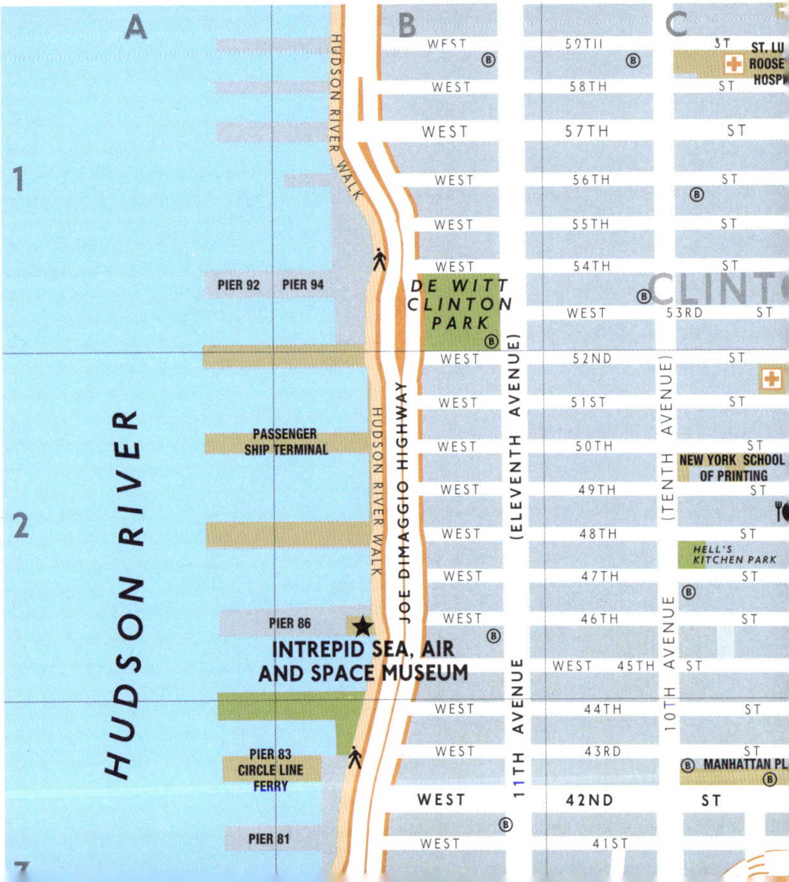

▶ Map F

D

Times Square / Theater District / Rockefeller Center

In the heart of the Theater District is Times Square, more brightly lit than ever before, with giant billboards, huge neon signs and illuminated newsboards. Of course, there's as much to see on the streets as on stage. On New Year's Eve hundreds of thousands of people congregate here to watch the crystal ball drop 77 feet at midnight. Further east on 42nd, behind the Public Library, is Bryant Park; in the summer, bring a blanket and watch a movie on the 20 by 40 ft screen.

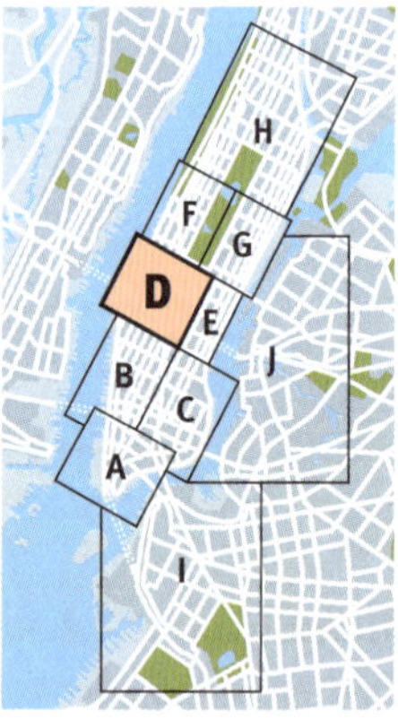

GAZALA'S PLACE

IPPUDO

RESTAURANTS

Joe Allen (D2) 1
→ *326 W 46th St (Eighth and Ninth); Tel. (212) 581 6464; Daily noon (11.30am Wed, Sat-Sun)–11.45pm (midnight Fri-Sat)*
Posters hang on the brick walls of this spot which caters to actors and theater-goers alike. Hamburgers, steaks, spare-ribs and fish are served until late in a cozy room with a big bar. Burgers $15; entrées $20–36.

Gazala's Place (C2) 2
→ *709 Ninth Ave (49th) Tel. (212) 245 0709 Daily 11am–11pm (11.30pm Fri-Sat)*
Chef/owner Gazala Halabi cooks up her native Druze cuisine. Also at 380 Columbus Ave (78th). Entrées $12.50–19.50.

Orso (D2) 3
→ *322 W 46th St (Eighth and Ninth); Tel. (212) 489 7212; Daily noon (11.30am Wed, Sat-Sun)–11.45pm*
This small northern Italian restaurant often has a Broadway star or director after the show. The crisp pizza bread with garlic is irresistible, as are the small crunchy pizzas and pan-roasted chicken. Service is quick and friendly. Entrées $15–29.

DB Bistro Moderne (E2) 4
→ *55 W 44th St (Fifth and Sixth); Tel. (212) 391 2400 Mon-Fri 7–10am, 11.30am–2.30pm, 5–11pm (10pm Mon); Sat-Sun 8am–2.30pm, 5–11pm (10pm Sun)*
In the fancier back or in the casual front room, try the burger with foie gras and truffles. Three-course pre-theater prix fixe $50; entrées from $29.

Ippudo (D2) 5
→ *321 W 51st St (Eighth and Ninth) Tel. (212) 974 2500 Daily 11am–3.30pm, 5–11.30pm (12.30am Fri-Sat)*
Delicious appetizers and ramen in this attractive setting of red banquettes set against brick walls or at the long, blond wood bar. Also at 65 Fourth Ave. Entrées $15–18.

The Modern (F1) 6
→ *9 W 53rd St (Fifth) Tel. (212) 333 1220; Mon-Sat noon–2pm, 5–10.30pm Bar Room: Daily 11.30am–10.30pm (9.30pm Sun)*
Bauhaus meets Danish Modern in the formal Dining Room and in the casual Bar Room, where mixing your menu is part of the fun: spicy steak

ROADWAY THEATER

MIDTOWN COMICS

ANTHROPOLOGIE

tartare with quail egg, for example. Small plates from $12 (Bar Room); prix fixe (dinner) $98–128.

CAFÉS, TEAROOMS

Café Un Deux Trois (E2) 7
→ *123 W 44th St (Broadway and Sixth); Tel. (212) 354 4148; Daily 7am–midnight*
This bistro has a vast bar where you can get a snack too. Friendly service.

Amy's Bread (D2) 8
→ *672 Ninth Ave (47th)*
Tel. (212) 977 2670; Mon-Wed 7am–10pm (9pm Mon); Thu-Fri 7am–11pm; Sat-Sun 8am–11pm (9pm Sun)
A popular neighborhood bakery with amazing cookies and artisanal breads.

Lady M (E3) 9
→ *36 W 40th St*
Tel. (212) 452 2222; Mon-Fri 9am–8pm (10pm Fri); Sat-Sun 11am–10pm (6pm Sun)
Pattisserie renowned for its 'mille crêpes', cakes made up of 20 layers of wafer-thin crêpes and cream in a dizzying variety of flavors.

Maison Kayser (D1) 10
→ *1800 Broadway (Columbus Circle)*
Tel. (212) 245 4100
Daily 7am–10pm
Ideal for a coffee or tea and a French pastry in their bright, cozy space.

Dean & DeLuca Cafe (F2) 11
→ *1 Rockefeller Plaza (48th St); Tel. (212) 664 137*
Mon-Fri 7am–7pm;
Sat-Sun 9am–5pm
Next to Rockefeller Center, a perfect spot for an espresso and pastry break.

THEATERS, BAR, CLUBS

Broadway theaters (D1-E3) 12
→ *See Welcome to New York*
They are on Broadway between 42nd and 53rd streets, or the side streets usually between Broadway and Eighth.

SixtyFive at the Rainbow Room (E2) 13
→ *30 Rockefeller Plaza*
Tel. (212) 632 5000
Mon-Fri 5pm–midnight
Enjoy the spectacular view and the spicy tuna tacos or the langoustine tartare with your drinks.

The Lambs Club (E3) 14
→ *132 W 44th St (Broadway and Sixth)*
Tel. (212) 997 5262
Daily 7am–2.30pm (3pm Sat-Sun), 5–11pm (9.30pm Sun-Mon)
Now the Chatwal Hotel, this 1905 Sanford White building once housed America's first theatrical club. The bar has an updated Deco look in red leather, metal and wood.

The Iridium (D2) 15
→ *1650 Broadway (51st)*
Tel. (212) 582 2121
Daily 7pm–midnight; nightly shows 8.30pm, 10.30pm
Excellent jazz club with American food. Cover charge $25–60.

SHOPPING

Anne Fontaine (F2) 16
→ *610 Fifth Ave (Rockefeller Center)*
Tel. (212) 489 1554
Mon-Fri 10am–7pm; Sat 11am–6pm; Sun noon–5pm
In case you need an iconic white blouse, this is the place to get it. Also at 873 Madison Ave and 93 Greene St.

Macy's (E4) 17
→ *151 W 34th St (Broadway)*
Tel. (212) 695 4400
Mon-Sat 10am–10pm (11pm Fri-Sat); Sun 11am–9pm
This vast department store has the usual goods, but at reasonable prices.

B & H (D4) 18
→ *420 Ninth Ave (34th)*
Tel. (212) 615 8820
Mon-Fri 9am–7pm (2pm Fri); Sun 10am–6pm
The largest audiovisual shop in New York: video, photographic and computer goods at very reasonable prices.

Midtown Comics (E3) 19
→ *200 W 40th St (Seventh)*
Tel. (212) 302 8192
Mon-Sat 8am–midnight; Sun noon–8pm
Graphic novels, books, comics; also T-shirts, masks, models, costumes and videos.

Hell's Kitchen Flea Market (C3) 20
→ *W 39th St (Ninth Ave)*
Sat-Sun 9am–5pm
There are finds: clothes, vintage jewelry, antiques.

Anthropologie (F2) 21
→ *50 Rockefeller Plaza*
Tel. (212) 246 0386
Daily 10am–9pm (8pm Sun)
Ethnic-inspired fashion: colorful clothes, jewelry, perfume, candles, shoes, bags and accessories.

MoMA Design Store (E1) 22
→ *44 W 53rd St (Fifth and Sixth)*
Tel. (212) 767 1050
Daily 9.30am–6.30pm (9pm Fri)
State-of-the-art gadgets and art posters from the 1940s–70s; also crockery and some furniture. Also at 81 Spring St.

ES SQUARE

MADAME TUSSAUDS

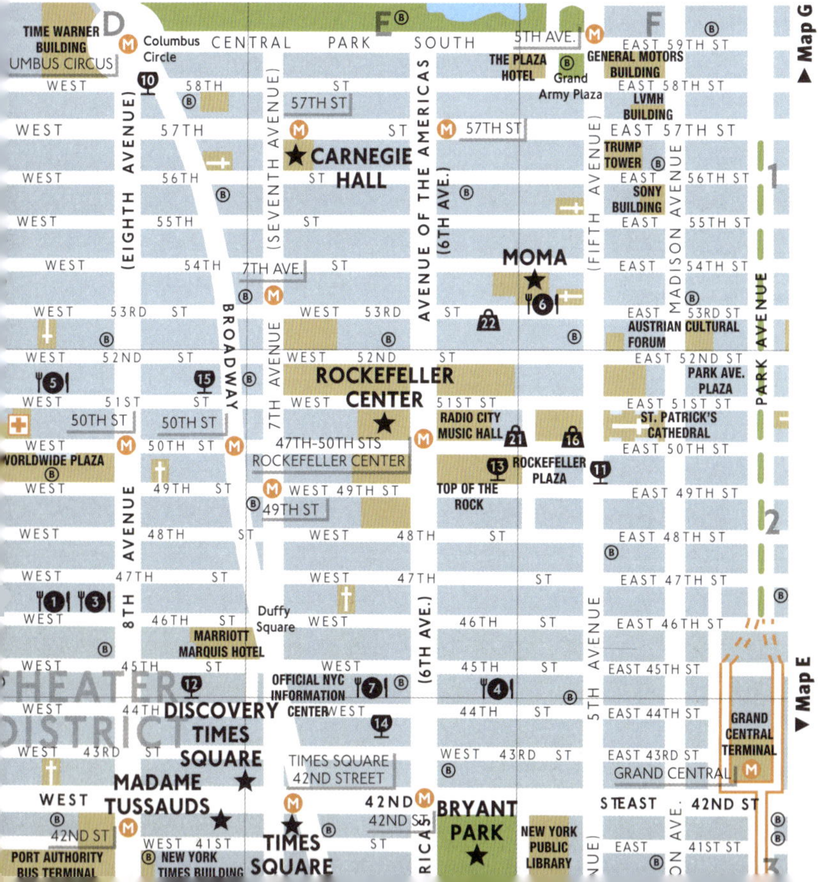

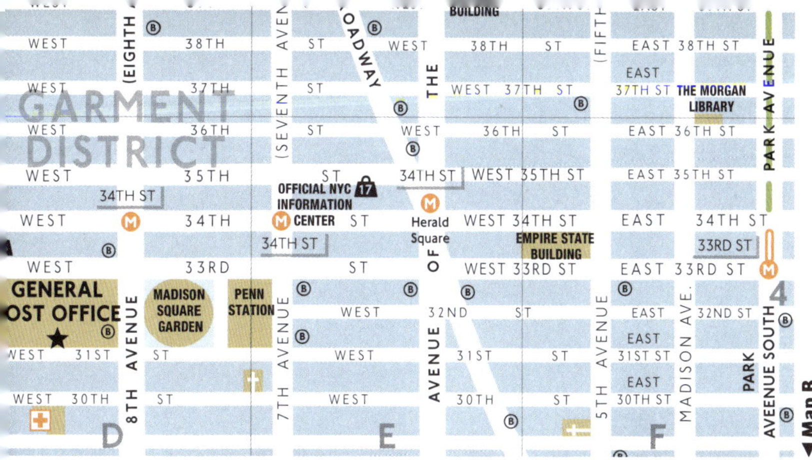

MUSEUM OF MODERN ART (MOMA)

CARNEGIE HALL

rs (daily 11am–3pm, every mins); box office: Mon-Sat m–6pm
ened in 1932 in the sence of Charlie aplin, Clark Gable and uro Toscanini, Radio y, with its 5,800-seat ditorium, is one of the st dramatic spaces in w York. The restored erior of the building is Art Deco masterpiece.

Intrepid Sea, Air and ace Museum (B2)
Pier 86, 12th Ave th St); Tel. (212) 245 0072 ly 10am–5pm m Sat-Sun from April-Oct)
4s, F-16s, planes from rld War Two and Hueys from Vietnam are part of the restored aircraft carrier museum; don't miss the Concorde or the Space Shuttle. Many interactive exhibits.

★ Museum of Modern Art (MoMA) (F1)
→ 11 W 53rd St
Tel. (212) 708 9400
Daily 10.30am–5.30pm (8pm Fri)
Yoshio Taniguchi's rebuilding of the museum has doubled the space of this great collection, which includes masterpieces of Fauvism, post-Impressionism, Cubism and Surrealism, as well as of photography and design.

★ Carnegie Hall (E1)
→ 881 Seventh Ave (57th)
Tel. (212) 247 7800
Guided tours: Oct-June: Mon-Fri 11.30am, 12.30pm, 2pm, 3pm; Sat 11.30am, 12.30pm; Sun 12.30pm (varies by week, check beforehand)
Built for steel magnate Andrew Carnegie, this is New York's oldest concert hall and its most perfect, acoustically. It opened in 1891 with Tchaikovsky conducting. Some of the biggest names in music have performed here, from Caruso, Toscanini and Von Karajan to The Beatles. The smaller Zankel Hall is on the lower level.

★ Discovery Times Square (D3)
→ 226 W 44th (Broadway and Eighth Ave); Tel. (866) 987 9692; Daily 10am–7pm (8pm Wed-Thu; 9pm Fri-Sat)
A vast 60,000 sq-ft museum-like space with educational, entertaining and interactive exhibitions such as: Titanic, Leonardo da Vinci's Workshop, King Tut, Terracotta Warriors and The Hunger Games.

★ Hudson Yards (C4)
→ 30-34th St (10th Ave)
Thomas Heatherwick's Vessel that rises to 15 stories, filled with 2,500 steps to climb in the 5-acre garden and plaza.

GRAND CENTRAL TERMINAL

CHRYSLER BUILDING

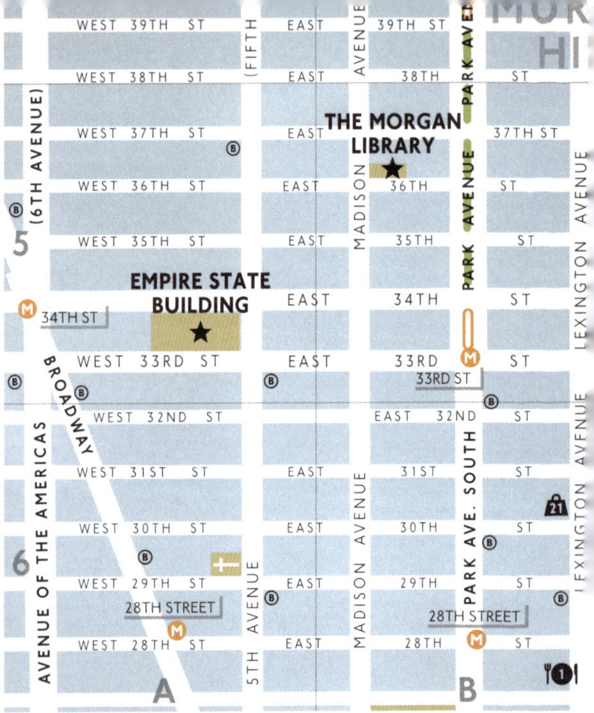

★ Empire State Building (A5)
→ *350 Fifth Ave*
Tel. (212) 736 3100
Daily 8am–2am
The construction of this legendary skyscraper in 1930 – then the highest ever man-made building – took 411 days and cost $42 million. The top mast initially served as a mooring place for airships. Until 1 WTC, it was the tallest building in the city (at 1,454 ft) and it still draws over 3.6 million visitors a year who come to see the views of downtown Manhattan and Central Park from its observatories on the 86th and 102nd floors.

★ New York Public Library (A4)
→ *Fifth Ave (42nd)*
Tel. (917) 275 6975
Mon-Sat 10am–6pm (8pm Tue-Wed); Sun 1–5pm
With 11 million books catalogued, this is the third largest public library in the US, after Washington's Library of Congress and Boston. Designed by the Beaux Arts architects John M. Carrère and Thomas Hastings, it opened in 1911. The stairway of this stunning building, guarded by two stone lions, is a favorite meeting place.

★ Villard Mansions (B2)
→ *451–457 Madison Ave (50th and 51st)*
These buildings, with the look of a Renaissance palace, were built in 1885 to fulfill the grand dreams of Henry Villard, founder of the Northern Pacific Railway. They now house the Palace Hotel.

★ The Morgan Library (B5)
→ *225 Madison Ave (36th)*
Tel. (212) 685 0008
Tue-Fri 10.30am–5pm (9pm Fri); Sat-Sun 10am (11am Sun)–6pm
Renzo Piano redesigned part of this space with its marvelous collection of medieval and Renaissar manuscripts, rare books and old master drawings financier J. Pierpont Morg (1837–1913), on display a neo-Renaissance pala dating from 1906.

★ Grand Central Terminal (B4)
→ *42nd St (Park Ave)*
This Beaux Arts building completed in 1913, brou the railway right into the heart of Manhattan, and now over 750,000 commuters pass throug every day. The spectacu main marble hall (375 ft long, 120 ft wide) has a gorgeous ceiling with th

EMPIRE STATE BUILDING

THE MORGAN LIBRARY

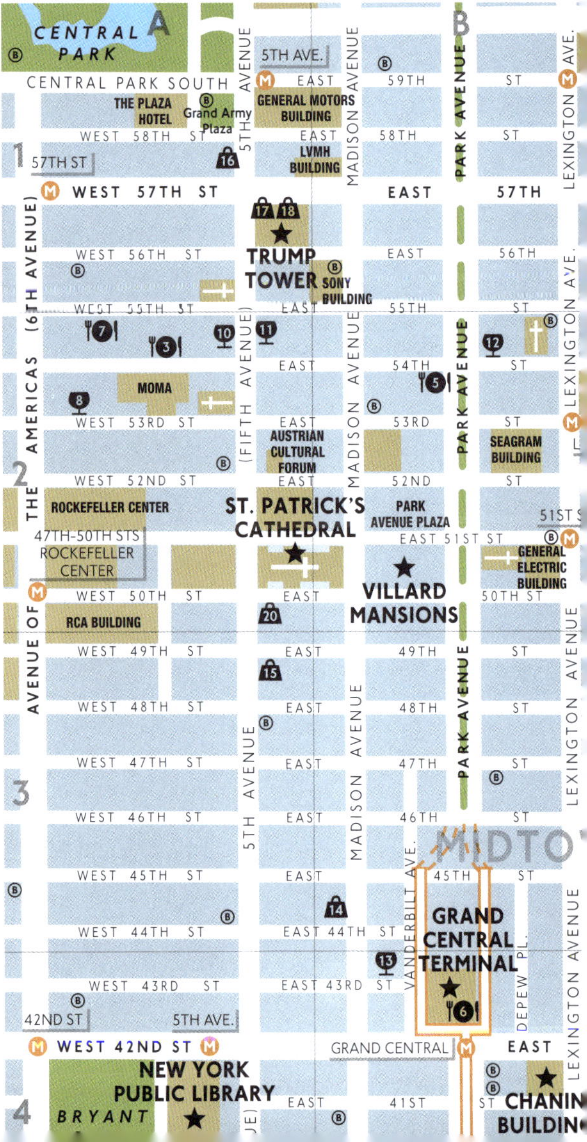

▲ Map D

From the Morgan Library & Museum on 36th and Madison, designed by Charles McKim with a Renzo Piano addition, stroll over to Fifth Avenue past the lions in front of The New York Public Library and take a right on 42nd Street to see Art Deco Chanin and Chrysler Buildings on Lexington Avenue. Walk through Grand Central Station, with its many shops, over to Fifth Avenue past the Channel Gardens of Rockefeller Center and up to the shopping district beyond the spires of St Patrick's Cathedral.

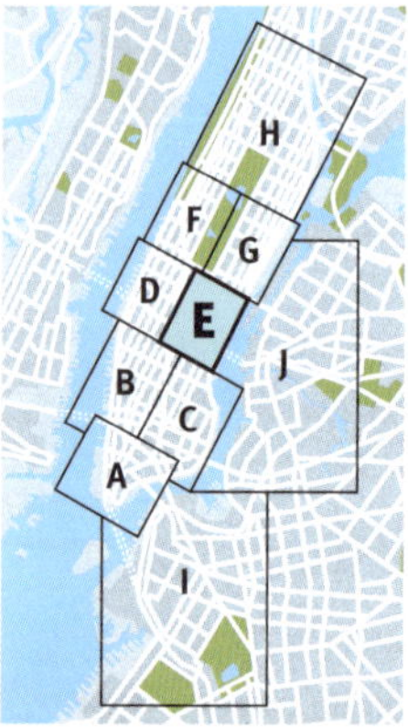

PONGAL

GRAND CENTRAL OYSTER BAR

RESTAURANTS

Pongal (B6) 1
→ *110 Lexington Ave (27th and 28th); Tel. (212) 696 9458; Daily noon–10pm*
A cozy restaurant offering authentic vegetarian cuisine from the south of India. Entrées $9–13.

Sushi Yasuda (C4) 2
→ *204 E 43rd St (Second and Third); Tel. (212) 972 1001; Mon-Fri noon–2.15pm, 6–10.15pm; Sat 6–10.15pm*
An elegant floor-to-ceiling bamboo space with great sushi. Entrées $20–38.

Il Gattopardo (A2) 3
→ *13-15 W 54th (Fifth and Sixth); Tel. (212) 246 0412 Daily noon (11.30am Sat-Sun)–3pm, 5–11.30pm (10pm Sun)*
At this Neapolitan restaurant try the pastas or poached filets of wild bass over a crispy salad and espresso granita for dessert. Entrées from $28.

Mr. Chow (C1) 4
→ *324 E 57th St (First and Second); Tel. (212) 751 9030 Daily 6–11.30pm*
The Richard Smith sculpture suspended over the sunken dining room, all mirrors and black lacquer, makes a stylish setting for eating Chinese food. Noodles $13; other entrées $27. Also at 121 Hudson St.

Casa Lever (B2) 5
→ *390 Park Ave (54th St) Tel. (212) 888 2700; Daily 7am (5.30pm Sat)–11pm*
In a room with Warhol portraits, sink into a booth for Milanese fare; weather permitting, have a drink or eat outside. Entrées $29–49.

Grand Central Oyster Bar (B4) 6
→ *Grand Central Terminal, lower level Tel. (212) 490 6650 Mon-Sat 11.30am–9.30pm*
Seafood specialties in a spectacular Beaux Arts vaulted, tiled underground space. Entrées $18–42.

Michael's (A2) 7
→ *24 W 55th St (Sixth) Tel. (212) 767 0555 Mon-Fri 7.30–9.30am, noon–2.30pm, 5.30–9.30pm; Sat 5.30–9.30pm*
Eavesdrop on the next big media merger while enjoying upscale Californian cuisine at this airy power spot with unparalleled people-watching. Entrées $18–48.

BARS

B Bar at Baccarat Hotel (A2) 8
→ *28 West 53rd (Fifth and*

RAND CENTRAL MARKET

BERGDORF GOODMAN

NIKE TOWN

Sixth); Tel. 212 790 8800; Daily 4pm–midnight
Under crystal chandeliers, have drinks with spicy tuna tartare, truffled French fries, foie gras or desserts; also has an outside terrace and the Salon for drinks or tea.

P. J. Clarke's (C1) 9
→ *915 3rd Ave (55th) Tel. (212) 317 1616; Daily 11.30am–4am (kitchen 3am)*
Since 1884, a lively bar now famous for its hamburgers and cheesecake.

Salon de Ning (A2) 10
→ *The Peninsula Hotel, 700 Fifth Ave (55th) Tel. (212) 903 3097; Daily 5pm–1am (midnight Sun)*
On the 23rd floor of the Peninsula Hotel, this bar evokes 1930s Shanghai inside and outdoors; Asian-inspired light fare and a great midtown view.

King Cole Bar & Salon (A2) 11
→ *The St Regis Hotel, 2 E 55th St (Fifth) Tel. (212) 339 6857 Mon-Sat 11.30am–1am; Sun noon–midnight*
This bar, with the famous Maxfield Parrish mural, has been expanded into a lounge where you can also get breakfast, lunch and dinner.

Monkey Bar (B2) 12
→ *60 East 54th St (Park Ave); Tel. (212) 288 1010 Mon-Fri 11.30am–1am; Sat 5.30pm–1am*
A cozy bar with the original monkey murals, at banquettes you can grab a bite off the main menu (entrées from $22).

The Campbell Apartment (B4) 13
→ *15 Vanderbilt Ave (43rd St); Tel. (212) 297 1781 Daily noon–2am*
This room with 25-foot ceilings channelling a 13th-century Florentine palazzo once owned by a 1920s tycoon is a great place to have a drink.

SHOPPING

Brooks Brothers (B3) 14
→ *346 Madison Ave (44th) Tel. (212) 682 8800 Mon-Fri 8am–8pm; Sat 9am–7pm; Sun 11am–7pm*
The place for classic suits, ties, pajamas and shirts; also children's clothes (ages 5–16) and preppy women's clothing.

Saks Fifth Avenue (A3) 15
→ *611 Fifth Ave (49th) Tel. (212) 753 4000 Mon-Sat 10am–8.30pm; Sun 11am–7pm*
The latest styles from the top designers and an excellent selection of cosmetics and accessories.

Bergdorf Goodman (A1) 16
→ *754 Fifth Ave (58th) Tel. (212) 753 7300 Mon-Sat 10am–8pm; Sun 11am–7pm*
A luxurious department store selling American and international design: women's clothing (the men's store is across the street), baby clothes, antiques, linens and cosmetics.

Tiffany & Co (A1) 17
→ *727 Fifth Ave (57th) Tel. (212) 755 8000; Mon-Sat 10am–7pm; Sun noon–6pm*
A New York institution since 1837, and forever linked with the image of Audrey Hepburn looking through its window. Fine jewelry, china, crystal and tableware are all here.

Niketown (A1) 18
→ *6 E 57th St (Fifth) Tel. (212) 891 6453; Daily 10am (11am Sun)–8pm*
Four floors dedicated to Nike sportswear and shoes.

Grand Central Market (B4) 19
→ *Lexington Ave (42nd) Mon-Fri 7am–9pm; Sat 10am–7pm; Sun 11am–6pm*
In one hall of the station, find food for picnics – fully prepared – as well as cheeses, salamis and breads; also stores like L'Occitane, Swatch and Papyrus. Don't miss the Great Northern food hall.

Fifth Avenue stores (A1-5) 20
Some of the popular shops here are:
H&M (nos 505 and 589)
→ *Tel. (855) 466 7467*
Uniqlo (no. 666)
→ *Tel. (877) 486 4756*
Zara (no. 666)
→ *Tel. (212) 765 0477*
Bottega Veneta (no. 699)
→ *Tel. (212) 371 5511*
Dolce & Gabbana (no. 717)
→ *Tel. (212) 897 9653*
Armani (no. 717)
→ *Tel. (212) 209 3500*
Abercrombie & Fitch (no. 720)
→ *Tel. (212) 306 0936*
Gucci (no. 725)
→ *Tel. (212) 826 2600*

Dover Street Market (B6) 21
→ *160 Lexington Ave (30th St); Tel. (646) 837 7750; Daily 11am–7pm (noon–6pm Sun)*
Seven floors curated by Rei Kawakubo of Comme des Garcons with a mix of hip young and established designers; Rose Bakery for breakfast or lunch.

▶ Map G

CHANIN BUILDING

UNITED NATIONS

▼ Map J

VILLARD MANSIONS

ST PATRICK'S CATHEDRAL

TRUMP TOWER

◀ Map C

nstellations painted Paul Helleu in 1912 – rticularly impressive night when the stars ght up.

Chrysler Building (B4)
405 Lexington Ave
en during office hours
e steel spire of this ilding has become e of the symbols of New rk. Erected by William n Alen for the car agnate Walter Chrysler, is flamboyant Art eco building (1930) is mous for its gargoyles otographed by Margaret urke-White. Marble, rome-plated steel, anite and wood inlaid with floral motifs decorate its splendid lobby.

★ **United Nations** (D3)
→ *First Ave (46th)*
Tel. (212) 963 4475
Mon-Fri 9am–4.45pm; Sat-Sun 10am–4.45pm (guided tours weekdays only)
John D. Rockefeller, Jr donated 18 acres of land running alongside the East River, purchased for $8.5 million. The complex was built after World War II by a team of 11 architects, including Le Corbusier. A visit takes in the Security Council Chamber, the General Assembly Building and more. Watch out for Foucault's Pendulum, Norman Rockwell's mosaic and Chagall's stained-glass window in the lobby.

★ **Chanin Building** (B4)
→ *122 E 42nd St (Lexington)*
Another standout of New York's Art Deco architecture, this 1928 building is embellished with magnificent bronze friezes on the theme of evolution.

★ **St Patrick's Cathedral** (A2)
→ *50th St (Fifth Ave)*
Tel. (212) 753 2261
Daily 6.30am–8.45pm (no visits during services)
This Gothic building, the largest Catholic cathedral in the US (holds up to 2,400 people), was built for New York's vast Irish community and is now the starting point for the city's Easter and St Patrick's Day parades.

★ **Trump Tower** (A1)
→ *725 Fifth Ave (57th)*
Daily 8am–10pm
The work of real estate developer, now President, Donald Trump, this 68-story luxury tower built in 1983 has an Italian-marble paneled atrium and an 80-ft waterfall fountain. Heavy security makes going to the fifth floor for the tree-planted terrace hanging over the street impossible.

LINCOLN CENTER

AMERICAN FOLK ART MUSEUM

◀ Map D

★ **Columbus Circle** (C6)
→ *Southwest corner of Central Park*
The Time Warner building has changed the face of this area and draws visitors to its restaurants and mall with such stores as Stuart Weitzman and Diptyque.

★ **Maine Memorial** (C6)
→ *As above*
Sculpted by Attilio Picarelli, this bronze and marble Beaux Arts monument was erected by press tycoon William R. Hearst in 1913 to commemorate the US battleship Maine, sunk by the Spanish in 1898 in the harbor of Havana, which marked the beginning of the Spanish-American War.

★ **Museum of Arts and Design (MAD)** (C6)
→ *2 Columbus Circle (58th)*
Tel. (212) 299 7777
Tue-Sun 10am–6pm (9pm Thu-Fri)
Formerly the American Craft Museum designed by Edward Durrell-Stone, MAD recently moved to this building redesigned by Brad Cloepfil. The museum presents an overview of the latest trends in objects, furnishings and craft techniques. Great store for unusual gifts.

★ **Lincoln Center** (B5)
→ *70 Lincoln Plaza at Broadway (62nd and 65th)*
Tel. (212) 875 5456; Guided tours: daily 10.30am–4.30pm (times vary)
Diller Scofidio & Renfro brilliantly redid Alice Tully Hall, and many parts of this complex, also adding cinemas. The seven buildings dedicated to the performing arts hold up to 12,000 spectators. The main venues are the Metropolitan Opera House, David Geffen Hall (home to the New York Philharmonic orchestra), the Vivian Beaumont Theater, the David H. Koch Theater, Alice Tully Hall and the Juilliard School of Music.

★ **American Folk Art Museum** (C5)
→ *2 Lincoln Square (66th / Columbus Ave)*
Tel. (212) 595 9533
Tue-Sun 11.30am (noon Fri, Sun)–7pm (7.30pm Fri, 6pm Sun)
The fascinating permane collections and traveling exhibitions of American folk art: paintings, potte and fabrics from the 18th century to the present da

★ **The Dakota** (C4)
→ *72nd St (Central Park We*
A prestigious address which has been home

MAINE MEMORIAL

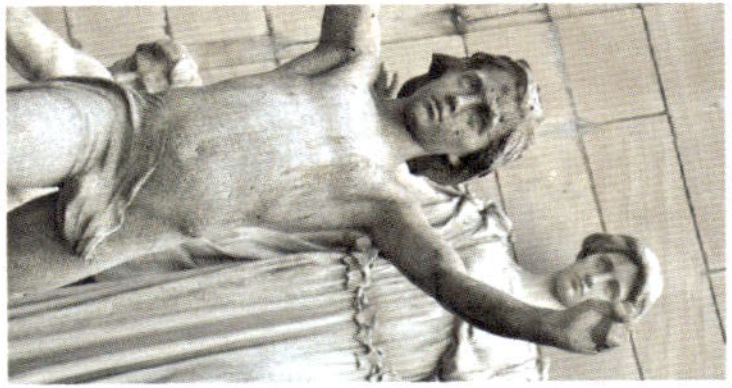

COLUMBUS CIRCLE

Immortalized by West Side Story, the upper west side has greatly changed since the period when Lincoln Center was being built (1955–69). Many of the big names in show business seem to prefer this luxurious but lively district to its equivalent across the Park. From Columbus Circle to 96th Street there are many good restaurants and bars to visit after seeing a show. From Lincoln Center you can take a short walk and visit the spectacular Rose Center for Earth and Space.

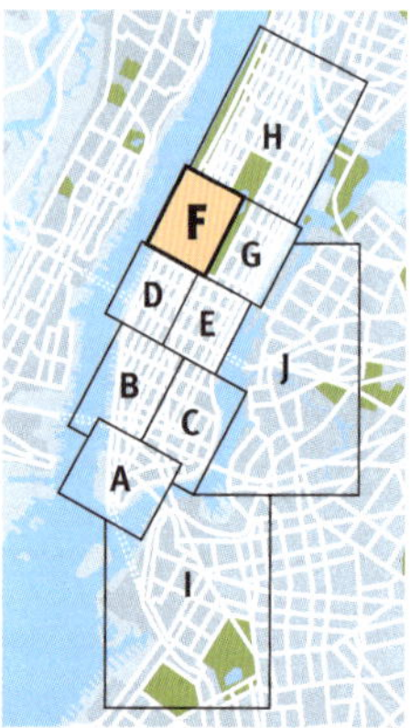

BARNEY GREENGRASS

CAFÉ LUXEMBOURG

RESTAURANTS

Blue Ribbon Sushi Bar & Grill (C6) 1
→ *6 Columbus Hotel, 308 W 58th St (Eighth)*
Tel. (212) 397 0404
Mon-Sat 7–10.30am, noon–2am; Sun noon–midnight
A beloved brand for classic sushi and cooked fish and meat. Downtown locations: 119 Sullivan St (**C** C5) and 187 Orchard St (**C** B4), and a brasserie at 97 Sullivan St (**C** C5). Entrées $15–33.

Salumeria Rosi (B4) 2
→ *283 Amsterdam Ave (74th); Tel. (212) 877 4800*
Mon-Fri noon–10pm; Sat-Sun 11am–11pm
Eat at the bar or at tables in this small, elegant spot; every kind of salumi and delicious pâtés and grilled vegetables. Small plates or platters $9–17.

Bar Boulud (C5) 3
→ *1900 Broadway (63rd and 64th)*
Tel. (212) 595 0303
Mon-Fri 11.30am–2.30pm, 5–11pm (midnight Fri); Sat-Sun 11am–4pm, 5–10pm (midnight Sat)
Across from Lincoln Center, this modern bistro with booths serves terrines, pâtés and coq au vin; next door Boulud Epicerie; on 64th, Boulud Sud for Mediterranean cuisine. Sandwiches from $16; entrées from $23 at Bar Boulud and Boulud Sud.

Barney Greengrass (B1) 4
→ *541 Amsterdam Ave (86th and 87th)*
Tel. (212) 724 4707
Tue-Sun 8am–6pm
A deli with formica tables and delicious smoked salmon, sturgeon bagels and East European specialties. Entrées from $11.

Café Luxembourg (B4) 5
→ *200 W 70th St (West End and Amsterdam)*
Tel. (212) 873 7411
Daily 8am (9am Sat-Sun)–midnight (11pm Sun-Tue)
Lynn Wagenknecht's 1930s-style bistro with a classic menu and a lively crowd of actors and writers. Entrées $25–40.

Nougatine at Jean-Georges (C6) 6
→ *1 Central Park West (60th and 61st)*
Tel. (212) 299 3900
Daily 7am (8am Sat-Sun)–10.30am, 11.45am–3.30pm, 5.30pm (5pm Fri-Sat)–11pm
In this modern space with a view of the park enjoy a crispy shrimp and avocado salad with

OM

BEACON THEATRE

ZABAR'S

champagne dressing. Three-course prix fixe (lunch) $38; dinner tasting menu $98.

Time Warner Center restaurants (C6) 7

→ *10 Columbus Circle*

Among the nine restaurants are Masa and Thomas Keller's Bouchon Bakery where you can sample (or take out) a sublime pastry, quiche or French-style baguette sandwich. And Whole Foods in the basement has salads, sushi and other take-out.

Shun Lee West (C5) 8

→ *43 W 65th St (Columbus and Central Park West)*
Tel. (212) 595 8895
Mon-Fri noon–midnight; Sat-Sun 11.30am–10.30pm (midnight Sat)

Popular with the Lincoln Center crowd. Attached is the black-and-white Shun Lee Café serving dim sum. Entrées $17–38 ($17 in the café).

ICE-CREAM PARLOR, CAFÉS

Maison Kayser (D6) 9

→ *1800 Broadway (59th St)*
Tel. (212) 245 4100
Daily 7am–10pm

A cozy café ideal for lunch, with tartines, sandwiches and salads – inside or out – and pre-theater dinner with onion soup, beef *bourguinon* and roasted salmon; also breakfast and brunch.

Grom (D6) 10

→ *1796 Broadway (58th and 59th); Tel. (212) 974 3444*
Daily 11am–11.30pm (12.30am Fri-Sat); opens noon Mon-Thu in winter

Extra-noir chocolate is just one of 20 ice-cream flavors from this Turin gelateria. Also at 233 Bleecker St (**B** C5).

Sarabeth's (B2) 11

→ *423 Amsterdam Ave (80th); Tel. (212) 496 6280*
Daily 8am–10pm

Great for breakfast, and the fruit juices are ambrosial.

BARS, CONCERTS

Lincoln Ristorante (B5) 12

→ *142 W 65th (Broadway and Amsterdam)*
Tel. (212) 359 6500
Mon-Tue 5–10.30pm; Wed-Fri noon–2pm, 5–10.30pm (11pm Thu-Fri); Sat-Sun 11.30am–2pm (2.30pm Sun), 5–11pm (9.30pm Sun)

Have a drink in the bar of this glass pavilion designed by Diller Scofidio + Renfro at Lincoln Center; in warm weather sit outside by the reflecting pool.

Beacon Theatre (B3) 13

→ *2124 Broadway (74th)*
Tel. (212) 465 6500
beacontheatre.com

A beautiful Art Deco theater which has hosted performers as varied as Leonard Cohen, Bruce Springsteen and Sting; see the concert program for upcoming shows.

The Office (C6) 14

→ *80 Columbus Circle (60th); Tel. (212) 805 8800*
Tue-Sat 4pm–midnight (1am Fri-Sat)

A small, intimate bar on the 35th floor of the Mandarin Oriental. The adjacent lobby lounge offers stunning views.

Jazz at Lincoln Center (C6) 15

→ *Time Warner Building, Frederick P. Rose Hall, (60th St and Broadway)*
Tickets from CenterCharge, daily 10am–9pm, tel. (212) 721 6500 or online: jazz.org

Special concerts at the Appel Room with its 50-ft glass wall overlooking the park (tickets $5–20 can be booked ahead). Listen to jazz nightly at:

Dizzy's Club Coca-Cola (C6) 16

→ *Tel. (212) 258 9595*
Concerts usually at 7.30pm and 9.30pm daily; entrance $20–45 plus $10 min. per person for food and drinks

SHOPPING

Zabar's (B2) 17

→ *2245 Broadway (80th)*
Tel. (212) 787 2000
Mon-Sat 8am–7.30pm (8pm Sat); Sun 9am–6pm

Gourmet food, ideal for picnics. Upstairs: kitchenware. Downstairs: fish, smoked meats, cheeses, pastries and rare teas.

J. Crew (C6) 18

→ *10 Columbus Circle*
Tel. (212) 823 9302
Daily 10am–9pm (7pm Sun)

Well-designed men's, women's and children's clothing, shoes and accessories.

Theory (C4) 19

→ *230 Columbus Ave (70th and 71st); Tel. (212) 362 3676*
Daily 10am (11am Sat)–7pm; Sun noon–6pm

Classic, popular women's clothes that are well cut and easy to wear.

Rag & Bone (C4) 20

→ *182 Columbus Ave (68th and 69th); Tel. 212 362 7138; Mon-Sat 11am–8pm; Sun noon–7pm*

Great jeans and hip casual tops, jackets, day and night wear.

▶ Map H

THE DAKOTA

STRAWBERRY FIELDS

NEW YORK HISTORICAL SOCIETY

▼ Map G

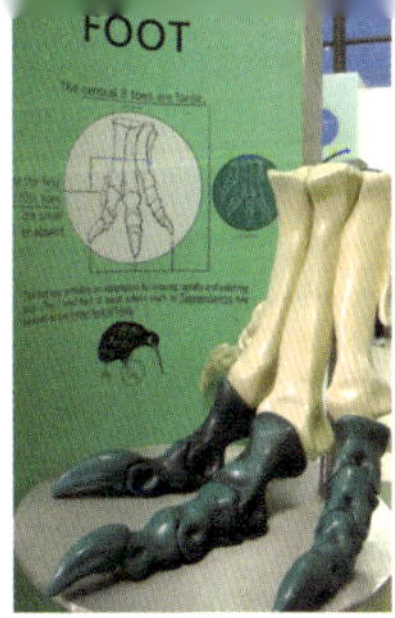

AMERICAN MUSEUM OF NATURAL HISTORY

RIVERSIDE PARK

a number of American
ars (Judy Garland,
uren Bacall, Boris Karloff,
onard Bernstein...).
ilt in 1884 by Edward
ark, president of Singer
wing Machines,
e Dakota was one of
w York's first luxury
artment buildings.
rmer Beatle John
nnon, who lived here,
s murdered just outside
December 8, 1980.
**Strawberry
elds** (D4)
72nd St (Central Park West)
this particularly bucolic
rner of Central Park
ing The Dakota, a
saic symbolizing peace, called Imagine, evokes one of John Lennon's greatest hits. Many fans still gather there to pay respects to his memory.

★ New York Historical Society (C3)
→ *170 Central Park West (77th); Tel. (212) 873 3400; Tue-Sat 10am–6pm (8pm Fri); Sun 11am–5pm*
New York's oldest museum, dating back to 1804, now renovated, has such attractions as a multimedia installation about New York's past, DiMenna's Children's History Museum and an Italian restaurant by Stephen Starr.

★ American Museum of Natural History (C3)
→ *Central Park West (79th St) (entrance by the Theodore Roosevelt Memorial)*
Tel. (212) 769 5100
Daily 10am–5.45pm
One of the largest natural history museums in the world has permanent exhibitions on minerals, dinosaurs, mammals, birds, and African, American-Indian and Asian civilizations. There are celebrated dioramas and first-rate temporary exhibits on everything from diamonds to live frogs and butterflies. Nature films are shown on a giant screen in the LeFrack Theater. Don't miss the fantastic planetarium next door: the Rose Center for Earth and Space.

★ Riverside Park (A3)
→ *Riverside Drive*
Running 86 blocks along the Hudson River, this is the second largest green expanse in Manhattan after Central Park. Frederick Law Olmsted followed the route of the Hudson River Railroad to create this vast park, which includes the Boat Basin Café at the end of 79th Street with an open-air space overlooking the marina.

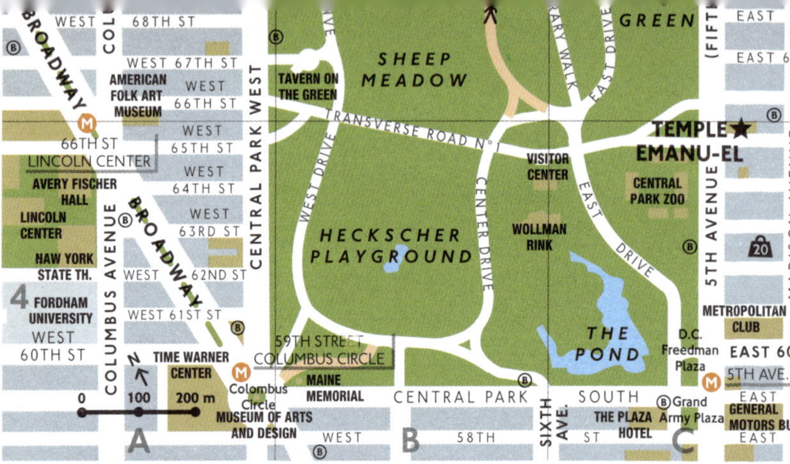

CENTRAL PARK

CENTRAL PARK ZOO

CENTRAL PARK / WOLLMAN RI

★ Central Park (B2)
→ *Visitor Center (65th St)*
Park open daily 6am–1am
Landscape architect Frederick Law Olmsted (1858–77) and Calvert Vaux designed the park in 1857. It took 20 years and 500,000 trees to create this 844-acre oasis in the middle of Manhattan.

Wollman Rink & Victorian Gardens (B4)
→ *East Drive (65th)*
Rink: Oct-April: daily 10am–10pm (2.30pm Mon-Tue, 11pm Fri-Sat, 9pm Sun); Gardens: End May-mid Sep: Daily 10am–7pm (times vary)
victoriangardensnyc.com
A mini amusement park with rides, slides, a roller-coaster in summer and open-air ice-skating in winter. Don't miss the Carousel at 64th St.

Central Park Zoo (C4)
→ *Fifth Ave (64th)*
Tel. (212) 439 6500; Daily 10am–5pm (5.30pm Sat-Sun); closes 4.30pm Nov-March
More than 150 species over the Tropic Zone, the Polar Circle and the open-air Temperate Territory; there is also a children's zoo. Don't miss the grizzly bear and snow leopards.

★ Roosevelt Island Tramway (E4)
→ *E 60th St (Second); Daily 6am–2.30am (3.30am Fri-Sat)*
Float over the East River in the aerial cable car, taking in the breathtaking panorama of the city for the price of a subway ticket.

★ Frick Collection (C3)
→ *One E 70th St (Fifth)*
Tel. (212) 288 0700; Tue-Sat 10am–6pm; Sun 11am–5pm
For nearly 40 years Henry Clay Frick, an industrialist from Pittsburgh, amassed a unique collection of artworks housed in his mansion: enamels from Limoges, Renaissance bronzes, paintings by Vermeer, Fragonard, Ingres, Bellini, El Greco and Whistler; and a collection of French royal furniture.

★ Mount Vernon Hote Museum & Garden (E4
→ *421 E 61st St (First)*
Tel. (212) 838 6878; Tue-Sun 11am–4pm (last tour 3.30pr
Built in 1799, this Federal style nine-room museum with 19th-century period furniture once belonged to President John Adams' daughter. Concerts in summer.

★ Temple Emanu-El (C4
→ *One E 65th St (Fifth)*
Tel. (212) 744 1400
Sun-Thu 10am–4.30pm
Built in 1929, this largest reformed synagogue in the world, a Byzantine-Romanesque-style templ

ROOSEVELT ISLAND TRAMWAY

MOUNT VERNON HOTEL MUSEUM & GARDEN

TEMPLE EMANU-EL

G

Upper East Side

Historically the home of the well-heeled, the luxurious and rather formal upper east side spreads across eight major streets. From west to east the first three are: Fifth Avenue, famous for its major museums, apartments with views of the Park and some of New York's most exclusive stores; Madison Avenue, lined with boutiques of the leading names in fashion; and the largely residential Park Avenue, with its pre-war apartment buildings, each guarded by diligent doormen.

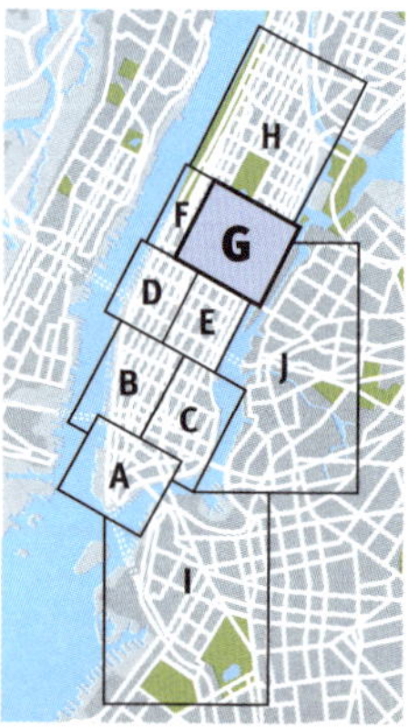

EJ'S LUNCHEONETTE

THE LOEB BOATHOUSE

RESTAURANTS

Sette Mezzo (D3) 1
→ *969 Lexington Ave (70th and 71st)*
Tel. (212) 472 0400
Daily noon–3pm, 5–11pm
Daily specials in a bustling atmosphere of neighborhood regulars. Sister restaurant, Vico is at 1302 Madison Ave (**H** D5). Entrées $25–43.

EJ's Luncheonette (D3) 2
→ *1271 3rd Ave (73rd)*
Tel. (212) 472 0600
Daily 7.30am–10pm (10.30pm Wed-Sat)
This popular spot has a classic American diner menu. Entrées $8–19.

Via Quadronno (C3) 3
→ *25 E 73rd St (Madison)*
Tel. (212) 650 9880
Mon-Sat 8am (9am Sat)–11pm; Sun 10am–9pm
This tiny Milanese restaurant has great espresso, delicious panini and salads. Panini from $7.50; entrées $20–38. Also at 1228 Madison Ave (**H** C6).

E. A. T. (C2) 4
→ *1064 Madison Ave (80th and 81st); Tel. (212) 772 0022; Daily 7am–10pm*
Refined deli food served in a soda fountain-style setting. Entrées $20–44.

The Mark Restaurant by Jean-Georges (C2) 5
→ *The Mark Hotel, 25 E 77th St (Madison); Tel. (212) 744 4300; Restaurant: daily 5.30pm–1am*
A lively bar leads to the restaurant where the favorites include black truffle pizza or the Mark cheeseburger; late dinner (until 1am). Entrées $29–58.

The Loeb Boathouse Central Park (B2) 6
→ *Central Park Lake (East Park and 72nd); Tel. (212) 517 2233; Mon-Fri noon–3.45pm, 5.30–9pm; Sat-Sun 9.30am–3.45pm, 6–9pm (not open for dinner Dec-March)*
In the Park, on the lake, try the roasted cornish game hen or bronzino; lunch and dinner. Entrées $24–47.

Sant Ambroeus (D2) 7
→ *1000 Madison Ave (78th) Tel. (212) 570 2211; Daily 7am (8am Sat-Sun)–11pm*
This Milanese spot serves breakfast, lunch and dinner, with amazing cakes, sandwiches, cookies and ice cream to go and an espresso bar. Entrées $26–66. Also at 61st St between Park and Madison (**G** D4), 1136 3rd

JB MACANUDO

ZITOMER

BLOOMINGDALE'S

Ave (**G** D3), 259 W 4th Street (**B** B3) and 265 Lafayette (**C** A5).

CAFÉS, BARS, CONCERTS

Flora Bar (D2) 8
→ *The Met Breuer, 945 Madison Ave (75th St) Tel. (646) 558 5383; Tue-Sun 11.30am–2.30pm, 5.30pm–10pm (11pm Fri-Sat)*
The partners of Café Altro Paradiso have created a lively space and outdoor patio. A light menu: some *crudo*, lamb's ribs with yogurt – among other offerings. Entrées $17–36.

Serendipity 3 (D4) 9
→ *225 E 60th St (Second and Third); Tel. (212) 838 3531; Daily 11.30am–midnight (1am Fri-Sat)*
Enjoy chicken sandwiches, hot dogs and hamburgers; and for dessert, their frozen hot chocolate or Forbidden Broadway Sundae, in a playful setting crammed with gadgets and toys for sale. Entrées from $17.

Maison Kayser (D2) 10
→ *1294 Third Ave (74th St) Tel. (212) 744 3100 Daily 7am–10pm*
This French bakery has more than 20 kinds of pastries; breakfast, lunch and dinner are also served; seven other locations in the city. Sandwiches from $13.

Café Carlyle (C2) 11
→ *35 E 76th St (Madison) Tel. (212) 744 1600 Mon-Sat 6.30–11pm*
Judy Collins and Woody Allen are among those who have performed at this small, elegant spot; Bemelmans Bar is across the hall.

Club Macanudo (C4) 12
→ *26 E 63rd St (Madison) Tel. (212) 752 8200 Daily noon–1am (2am Wed-Sat, 10pm Sun)*
Ideal for an evening drink and a cigar; dinner menu and Sunday brunch.

Ty Bar (B2) 13
→ *Four Seasons Hotel, 58 E 58th St (Madison and Park Ave); Tel. (212) 758 5700; Daily noon–1am (midnight Sun)*
Off the 57th Street lobby, a cozy setting with a fireplace and comfortable seating.

Park Avenue Armory (D3) 14
→ *643 Park Ave (66th and 67th); Tel. (212) 616 3030*
Built in 1861 as a military facility and social club, with rooms by Louis Comfort Tiffany, Stanford White and the Herter brothers, its 55,000-ft drill hall hosts concerts, plays and opera – Robert Wilson, Laurie Anderson, art installations by Paul McCarthy and art fairs.

SHOPPING

Roberta Roller Rabbit (D3) 15
→ *1019 Lexington Ave (73rd); Tel. (212) 772 7200 Mon-Sat 10am–6pm; Sun noon–5pm*
Colorful cotton tunics, dresses, beaded and woven bags, jewelry, curtains, bedding, tablemats and furniture – from India, South America and elsewhere.

Barneys (C4) 16
→ *660 Madison Ave (61st) Tel. (212) 826 8900 Mon-Sat 10am–8pm (7pm Sat); Sun 11am–7pm*
Nine stories dedicated to fashion, with accessories and cosmetics.

Zitomer (C2) 17
→ *969 Madison Ave (75th and 76th); Tel. (212) 737 5560; Mon-Sat 9am–8pm (7pm Sat); Sun 10am–6pm*
Great pharmacy with cosmetics on the main floor, accessories on the second and a toy store on the third.

Pretty Ballerinas (D2) 18
→ *1034 Lexington Ave (74th) Tel. (212) 249 7844 Mon-Fri 10am–7pm; Sat 11am–6pm; Sun noon–5pm*
A playful selection of ballerina-style flats ranging from $219–459.

Bloomingdale's (D4) 19
→ *1013 Lexington Ave (59th) Tel. (212) 705 2000 Mon-Sat 10am–8.30pm; Sun 11am–7pm*
This famous department store has everything, including day and evening wear, linens and hardware.

Fashion district (C4) 20
The heart of shopping for fashion and accessories.
→ **On 57th Street**
Louis Vuitton (no. 1), Saint Laurent (no. 3), Burberry (no. 9), Miu Miu (no. 11), Chanel (no. 15), Christian Dior (no. 21).
→ **On Madison Avenue**
Fendi (no. 598), Hermès (nos. 690, 691), Jimmy Choo (no. 699), Alice + Olivia (no. 755), Proenza Schouler (no. 822), Dolce & Gabbana (no. 827), Prada (no. 841), Ralph Lauren (nos. 867, 878, 888), Celine (no. 870), Christian Louboutin (no. 965-967), Vince (no. 980), among many others.

IA SOCIETY

FRICK COLLECTION

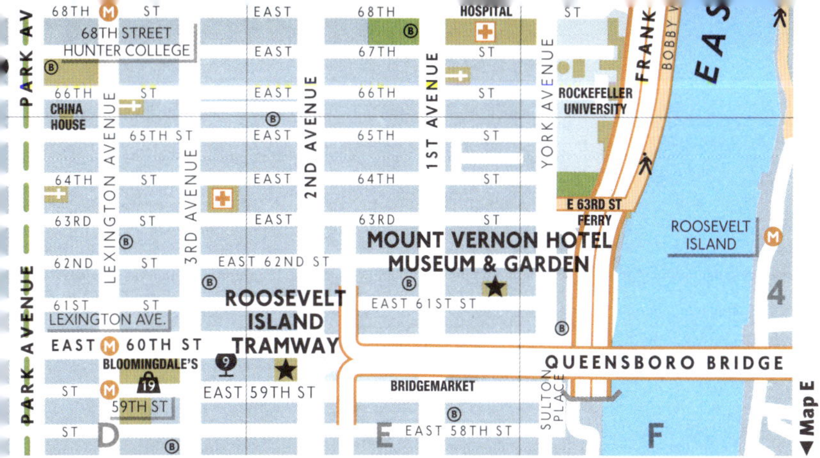

TROPOLITAN MUSEUM OF ART

GUGGENHEIM MUSEUM

ered with mosaics, its 2,500.

Asia Society (D3)
725 Park Ave (70th)
(212) 288 6400; Tue-Sun m–6pm (9pm Fri, except 1 through Labor Day)
me 300 pieces from John Rockefeller's superb ection: artifacts and rks of art from Japan, na and Afghanistan. ellent exhibitions.

Neue Galerie (C1)
048 Fifth Ave (86th)
(212) 628 6200
-Mon 11am–6pm
é Sabarsky: Wed-Mon n–6pm (9pm Thu-Sun)
rière & Hastings igned this 1914 building renovated as a museum for early 20th-century German and Austrian art and design. Klimt to the Wiener Werkstätte to the Blaue Reiter group are here. Café Sabarsky is run by the downtown restaurant Wallsé. Great bookstore.

★ Guggenheim Museum (C1)
→ 1071 Fifth Ave (89th)
Tel. (212) 423 3500; Fri-Wed 10am–5.45pm (7.45pm Sat)
Architect Frank Lloyd Wright designed the 2,624-ft gallery as a spiral climbing gradually upward toward the central dome. The permanent works here include the world's largest collection of Kandinskys, as well as an impressive number of Impressionist, Post-Impressionist and early modern masterpieces by Renoir, Degas, Monet, Van Gogh, Picasso and Léger; also sculptures by Calder, Giacometti and Brancusi.

★ Metropolitan Museum of Art (C1)
→ 1000 Fifth Ave (E 82nd)
Tel. (212) 535 7710; Daily 10am–5.30pm (9pm Fri, Sat)
Opened in 1872, this vast space holds more than two million works of art, among which great Italian works, an amazing collection of Egyptian and Roman antiquities and American art. The Temple of Dendur was shipped from Egypt and rebuilt stone by stone in the museum. See the 15 Islamic galleries and the renovated American Wing.

★ The Met Breuer (D2)
→ 945 Madison Avenue (75th)
Tue-Sun 10am–5.30pm (Thu-Fri 9pm)
metmuseum.org/metbreuer
The Metropolitan Museum of Art is curating contemporary exhibitions, performance works and interactive programs in this 1966 Marcel Breuer building, formerly the Whitney.

HARLEM MEER

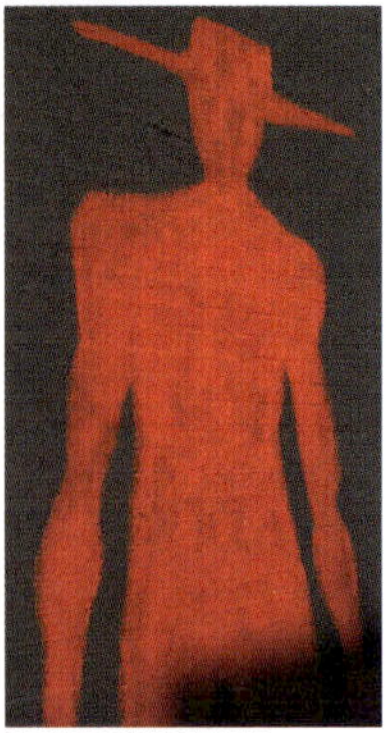

EAST HARLEM MURALS

★ **Cooper Hewitt, Smithsonian Design Museum** (C6)
→ *2 E 91st St (Fifth)*
Tel. (212) 849 8400
Daily 10am–6pm (9pm Sat)
Once the property of Andrew Carnegie, now the national design museum, the collection includes everything from wallpaper to architectural drawings and furniture. Much of the collection can be viewed through interactive software; a Models & Prototypes gallery illustrates the importance of models for design. There is a shop and the Taralucci café on the main floor.

★ **Museum of the City of New York** (C5)
→ *1220 Fifth Ave (103rd)*
Tel. (212) 534 1672
Daily 10am–6pm
A museum of the history and life of New York and its heroes, famous and unknown alike: historical documents, paintings, models, photos, posters, antique toys, famous dollhouses and costumes. Temporary exhibitions.

★ **Museo del Barrio** (C5)
→ *1230 Fifth Ave (104th)*
Tel. (212) 831 7272; Wed-Sat 11am–6pm; Sun noon–5pm
Founded in 1969, this museum presents films, lectures, temporary exhibitions and concerts all relating to Latin-American art and culture. Very pleasant café.

★ **St John the Divine Cathedral** (A4)
→ *1047 Amsterdam Ave (112th); Tel. (212) 316 7540*
Daily 7.30am–6pm (limited hours on Sundays)
Highlight tours: Mon 11am, 2pm; Tue-Sat 11am, 1pm; Sun 1pm (select weeks)
This enormous Gothic cathedral, begun in 1892, is still unfinished. Its central nave, a record 601 ft in length, leads to various chapels decorated by contemporary artists.

★ **Columbia University** (A3)
→ *Entrance on W 116th St a*
Broadway; Tel. (212) 854 49
Various tours offered Mon-F
This prestigious New York university occupies 36 acres between Broadway and Amsterdam. The new 17-acre Manhattanville campus is being built: th first project to have been completed is a 450,000-sq.-ft scientific research facility designed by Renz Piano.

★ **The Riverside Church** (A3)
→ *490 Riverside Drive (120*
Tel. (212) 870 6700
Daily 7am–10pm

◄ Map F

MUSEO DEL BARRIO

MUSEUM OF THE CITY OF NEW YORK

COOPER-HEWITT DESIGN MUSEUM

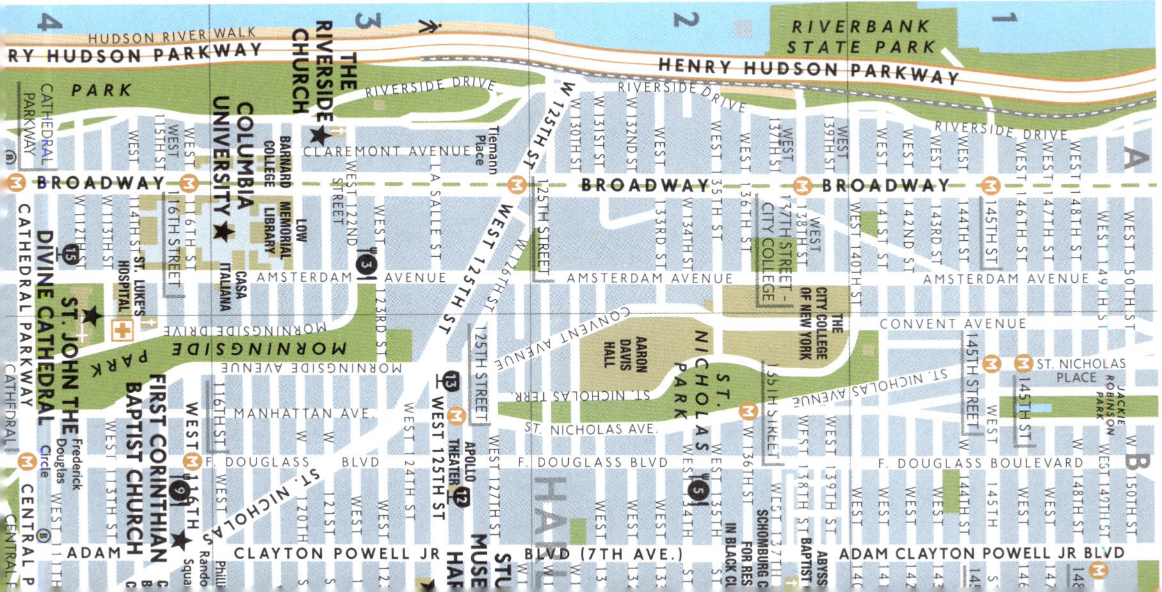

Heading north along upper Fifth Avenue, Museum Mile is home to some of New York's most famous museums: the Metropolitan, the Guggenheim, El Museo del Barrio... On the west side, once past the Museum of Natural History, a short taxi ride will take you to Morningside Heights, home to Columbia University and the vast Cathedral of St John the Divine. Further north is Harlem, historically home to New York's Afro-American community, gospel, jazz and real Southern cooking.

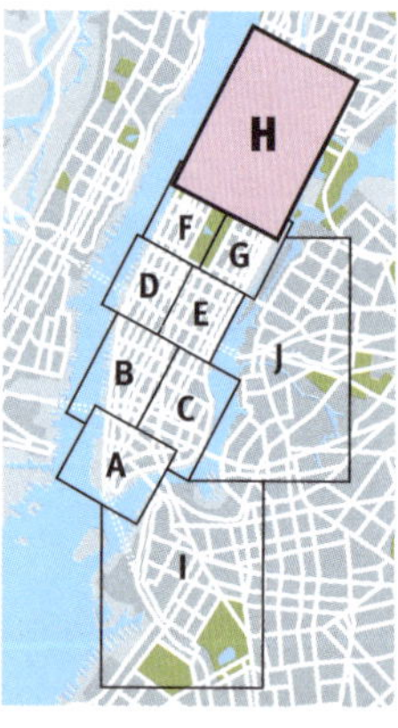

MAX SOHA

RED ROOSTER

RESTAURANTS

Elio's (D6) 1
→ *1621 Second Ave (84th)*
Tel. (212) 772 2242
Daily 5pm–midnight
This lively Italian restaurant serves a mean veal chop. On the walls are framed book jackets of authors who frequent it but so do media/movie types. Entrées $18–35.

Chez Lucienne (C3) 2
→ *308 Malcolm X Blvd (125th and 126th); Tel. (212) 289 5555; Mon-Fri 11am–midnight (2am Fri); Sat-Sun 9am–2am (11pm Sun)*
Settle into a banquette and enjoy French cooking – outside in fine weather; brunch and lunch, and live music on Saturdays. Entrées $14–26.

Max SoHa (A3) 3
→ *1274 Amsterdam Ave (123rd); Tel. (212) 531 2221*
Daily noon–midnight
Columbia University students love this trattoria's homemade pasta and chicken Marsala. Entrées $11–16.

Blvd Bistro (C3) 4
→ *239 Malcom X Blvd (122nd); Tel. (212) 678 6200*
Tue-Fri 5–11pm; Sat 11am–11pm; Sun 10am–6pm
In a charming, rustic townhouse, French-American bistro cooking: lunch and a few daily specials for dinner, including a great rib-eye steak. Entrées $16–30.

Abyssinia Ethiopian Restaurant (B2) 5
→ *268 W 135th St (Frederick Douglas Blvd); Tel: (212) 281 2673; Daily 11am–10pm*
Fans attest to the fantastic Ethiopian food cooked up by Daniel Rela and his wife in this 18-seat eatery. Entrées $13–21.

Red Rooster (C3) 6
→ *310 Lenox Ave (126th)*
Tel. (212) 792 9001
Mon-Fri 11.30am–3.30pm, 4.30–10.30pm (11.30pm Fri); Sat-Sun 10am–3pm, 4.30–11.30pm (10pm Sun)
Chef Marcus Samuelsson serves up Swedish meatballs and fried yard chicken in this bustling spot. Entrées from $18. Live music in Ginny's Supper Club in the basement.

Lenox Saphire (C3) 7
→ *341 Lenox Ave (127th St)*
Tel. (212) 866 9700
Daily 7am (8am Sat-Sun)–midnight (4am Fri-Sat)
On Thursdays you can hear Phil Young's friends play fantastic jazz and blues while you eat Senegalese-American

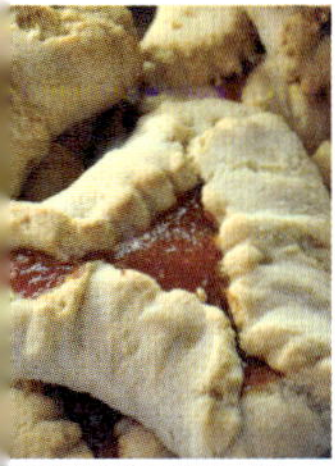

NGARIAN PASTRY SHOP

APOLLO THEATER

BLUE TREE

food: curries, stews or simply a burger or soul food. Entrées $11–16.

Sfoglia (D6) 8
→ 1402 Lexington Ave (92nd); Tel. (212) 831 1402
Mon-Tue 5.30–10pm (10.30pm Tue); Wed-Sun noon–2.30pm, 5.30–10.30pm (10pm Sun)
Rustic charm and Italian cooking; the fennel soup and squid ink risotto are memorable. Entrées $15–28.

Streetbird Rotisserie (B4) 9
→ 2149 Frederick Douglass Blvd (W 116th)
Tel. (212) 206 2557
Daily 11am–11pm
Chinese, Latin and El Barrio-influenced food in a setting inspired by 1970s–90s hip-hop. Entrées from $18.

CAFÉS, BARS, CONCERTS

Barawine (C3) 10
→ 200 Malcolm X Blvd (W 120th); Tel. (646) 756 4154; Mon-Fri 4–10pm (11pm Thu, Fri); Sat-Sun 11.30am–11pm (10pm Sun)
Enjoy a glass of wine and a niçoise salad or Black Angus carpaccio.

Smoke Jazz & Supper Club (A5) 11
→ 2751 Broadway (105th)
Tel. (212) 864 6662
Mon-Sat 5.30pm–3am; Sun 11am–3am
Cover charge $9–45
The jazz greats regularly play here in an atmosphere intimate, warm and totally without pretentions.

Apollo Theater (B3) 12
→ 253 W 125th St (Frederick Douglass Blvd)
Tel. (212) 531 5300
Guided tours: Mon, Tue, Thu, Fri 11am, 1pm, 3pm; Wed 11am; Sat-Sun 11am, 1pm
When it opened in 1913, this theater catered to a white audience, until 1934 when it opened its doors to black people. Many greats have performed here: Count Basie, Duke Ellington, Aretha Franklin, The Supremes and Stevie Wonder. 'Amateur night' on Wednesdays.

Showman's (B3) 13
→ 375 W 125th St (Morningside Ave)
Tel. (212) 864 8941
Mon-Sat 1pm–4am
Concerts: Wed-Thu 8.30pm, 10pm, 11.30pm; Fri-Sat 9.30pm, 11.30pm, 1.30am
Since 1942, this club has been the place to listen to live jazz. Weekly tap-dance night. No cover charge; minimum two drinks.

Noglu (C6) 14
→ 1266 Madison Ave (90th and 91st); Tel. (646) 895 9798
Mon-Sat 7.30am–7pm (7.30pm Sat); Sun 9am–5pm
This tearoom-pâtisserie has organic and gluten-free cakes, tarts, sandwiches and quiches.

Hungarian Pastry Shop (A4) 15
→ 1030 Amsterdam Ave (111th); Tel. (212) 866 4230
Mon-Sat 8am–11.30pm; Sun 8.30am–11pm
Columbia students like this old-world café for its pastries, hot chocolate, Viennese and Russian coffees. Cash only.

Sexy Taco Dirty Cash (C4) 16
→ 161 Malcolm X Blvd (118th); Tel. (212) 280 4700
Mon-Fri 4pm–midnight (1am Fri); Sat-Sun 11am–10pm (1am Sat)
A small, lively spot for a drink – margaritas, pacificos, wine and special cocktails.

SHOPPING

Carol's Daughter (C3) 17
→ 24 W 125th St (Lenox and Fifth)
Tel. (212) 828 6757
Mon-Sat 10am–8pm; Sun 11am–6pm; several outlets
Lisa Price's cosmetics – shampoos, soaps, oils, perfumes – made with natural ingredients.

Theory (C6) 18
→ 1157 Madison (85th and 86th)
Tel. (212) 879 0265
Mon-Sat 10am (11am Sat)–7pm; Sun noon–6pm
Great selection of their signature women's clothing; also men's.

Target (off D3) 19
→ 517 E 117th St (East River)
Tel. (212) 835 0860
Daily 8am–midnight (11pm Sun)
Inexpensive wares, from furniture, kitchen and bath products to dried food, jeans and designer collections.

Blue Tree (C6) 20
→ 1283 Madison Ave (92nd); Tel. (212) 369 2583
Mon-Sat 10am (11am Sat)–6pm
Actress Phoebe Cates's shop has women's clothing, jewelry and bath products.

Malcolm Shabazz Harlem Market (C4) 21
→ 52 W 116th St (Lenox)
Tel. (212) 987 8131
Daily 10am–8pm
A colorful covered market in the heart of Harlem: masks, African craftwork, clothes, music and movie posters.

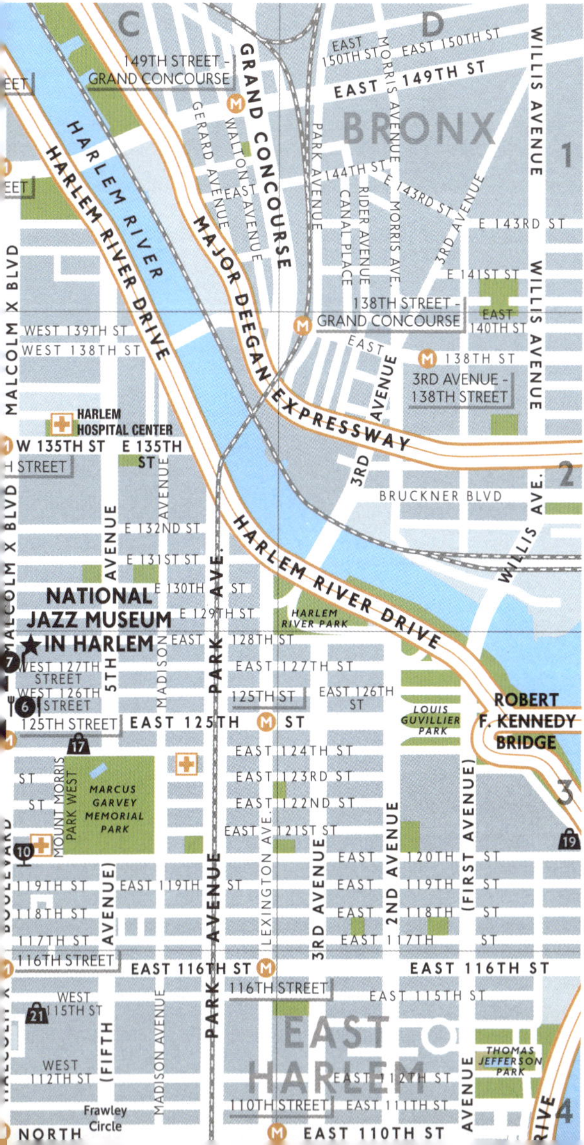

ST JOHN THE DIVINE CATHEDRAL

COLUMBIA UNIVERSITY

THE RIVERSIDE CHURCH

FIRST CORINTHIAN BAPTIST CHURCH

STUDIO MUSEUM IN HARLEM

◄ Map G

ınded in 1930 on the iative of J. D. Rockefeller, Riverside Church is othic-style building deled after Chartres hedral in France. Its antic 74-bell carillon ı its five-octave range ıe largest in the world.

★ First Corinthian ptist Church (B4)
→ *912 Adam Clayton vell Jr Blvd (Seventh)*
vices: Sun 7.30am, ɔam, 11.30am
ıst ornate church in former movie palace, Regent (1913), which embles a Venetian ıce. Visit on Sunday ıttend services and hear the glorious singing of the 70-member choir.

★ Studio Museum In Harlem (B3)
→ *144 W 125th St (Lenox Ave and Adam C. Powell Jr Blvd)*
Tel. (212) 864 4500
Thu–Sun noon (10am Sat)–6pm (9pm Thu–Fri)
This terrific museum of African-American arts has a large collection of paintings, sculpture and photographs, the latter including James Van Der Zee's work from the 1920s–30s Harlem Renaissance.

★ Harlem Meer (C4)
→ *Central Park (106th and 110th)*
Charles A. Dana Discovery Center: daily 10am–5pm
This lake in Central Park stretches from 106th to 110th Streets. There is catch-and-release fishing in summer and skating in the winter. It is also a good place to spot turtles and night herons.

★ East Harlem Murals (C5)
The walls of East Harlem can speak. Numerous colorful murals line the streets and avenues, one of the most famous being the four-story work created in the 1970s by Hank Prussing and Manny Vega, *The Spirit of East Harlem* (Lexington and 104th St). Also see the Graffiti Hall of Fame (106th/Park Ave), created in 1980, where well-known street artists display their skills on schoolyard walls.

★ National Jazz Museum in Harlem (C3)
→ *58 W 129th St*
Tel. (212) 348 8300
Thu–Mon 11am–5pm
An exciting collection of photographs, recordings, books and documentary film celebrating the jazz greats, from Duke Ellington to John Coltrane, via Charlie Parker. There are 1,000 records and DVDs available to listen to.

BROOKLYN HEIGHTS PROMENADE

BROOKLYN HISTORICAL SOCIETY

★ Manhattan Bridge (B1)
Manhattan's suspension bridge (1909, Leon Moisseiff) was the star of Sergio Leone's movie *Once Upon a Time in America,* and has a walkway and bikeway linking DUMBO to Chinatown.

★ Brooklyn Bridge (B1)
The initial plans, presented in 1855, seemed pure folly, and it wasn't until the end of the Civil War that the project saw the light of day. Some workers died during the 13 long years it took to build this steel suspension bridge, one of the longest and first of its kind in the world. A pedestrian walkway overlooks downtown, the East River and Brooklyn.

★ Brooklyn Heights Promenade (B2)
→ *Between Joralemon St and Grace Court*
This has to be the finest view of the Brooklyn Bridge and the skyscrapers of Lower Manhattan. Opened in 1950, the pedestrian walkway is a haven for joggers, artists looking for inspiration, and anyone admiring the sunset.

★ Brooklyn Bridge Park (B2)
→ *1 Main St; Daily 6am–1am*
An urban oasis located between the Brooklyn and Manhattan bridges, two riverside parks with views of the skyline. There are play areas, wild birds (with mulberry trees that attract them) and an old tobacco warehouse. Pier 1 has two large lawns and an imaginative children's playground.

★ Brooklyn Historical Society (B2)
→ *128 Pierrepont St (Clinton) Tel. (718) 222 4111 Wed-Sun noon–5pm*
Housed in a National Historic Landmark (1881) designed by George Post, with a fine, unglazed terracotta Queen Anne-style façade. The fourth floor is suspended, following the model of the Brooklyn Bridge. Inside, the museum documents Brooklyn's 400-year history.

★ New York Transit Museum (B3)
→ *Boerum Place (Schermerhorn); Tel. (718) 694 1600; Tue-Fri 10am–4pm; Sat-Sun 11am–5pm*
The entrance looks like a ordinary subway station but inside is an exhibitio tracing the history of the hundred-year-old netwo using photos, film footage and interactive installations (children ca

BROOKLYN BRIDGE PARK

BROOKLYN BRIDGE

MANHATTAN BRIDGE

I

Brooklyn Heights / DUMBO / BoCoCa / Park Slope

Brooklyn Heights, with its streets named after different fruit and its fine brownstone houses, has an old-fashioned provincial charm. To the north, DUMBO (Down Under the Manhattan Bridge Overpass) is home to a growing number of galleries and artistic communities housed in converted factories. To the east, young families and writers relax in cafés around BoCoCa (Boerum Hill, Cobble Hill and Carroll Gardens) and Park Slope, before heading off for a stroll in Prospect Park.

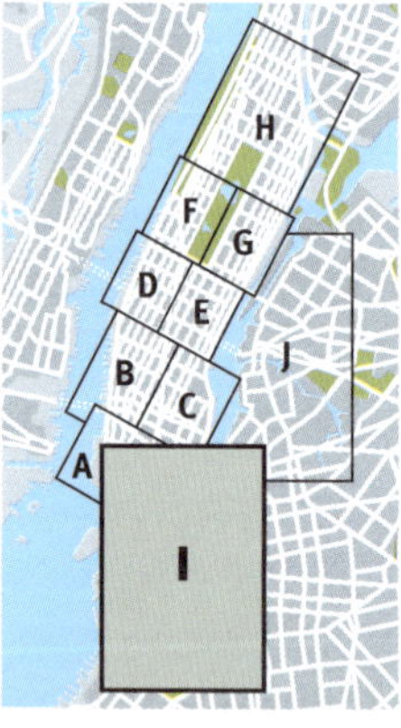

BUTTERMILK CHANNEL

RIVER CAFÉ

RESTAURANTS

Olmstead (D4) 1
→ *659 Vanderbilt Ave (Park & Prospect Place); Tel. (718) 552 2610; Daily 5–10.30pm*
Chef Greg Baxtrom has created a seasonal menu with greens and quail sourced from the garden out back. Entrees $13–24.

Lucali (A4) 2
→ *575 Henry St (Carroll) Tel. (718) 858 4086 Wed-Mon 6–10pm*
Seating 30, Mark Iacono serves up amazing pizza. No reservations; cash only. BYOB. Entrées $10–24.

Pok Pok (A3) 3
→ *127 Columbia St (Kane) Tel. (718) 923 9322; Daily 5.30 (Sat-Sun noon)–10.30pm*
Authentic Thai food including Chiang Mai sausages. No reservations. Entrées from $15.

Buttermilk Channel (A5) 4
→ *524 Court St (Huntington) Tel. (718) 852 8490 Daily 11.30am (10am Sat-Sun)–3pm, 5–10pm (11pm Thu, midnight Fri)*
Have the buttermilk-fried chicken with cheddar waffles in this light-filled room. Entrees $12–25.

Franny's (D4) 5
→ *348 Flatbush Ave (Sterling Pl and 8th Ave) Tel. (718) 230 0221 Mon-Thu 5.30–11pm; Fri noon–2.30pm, 5.30–11pm; Sat-Sun noon–11.30pm (10pm Sun)*
The best artisanal pizza; also organic salumi, appetizers, pasta and polenta – no entrées as such, as all is to share. $20–22.

River Café (B2) 6
→ *1 Water St Tel. (718) 522 5200; Mon-Fri 8.30–11.30am, 5.30–11pm; Sat-Sun 11.30am–2.30pm, 5.30–11pm*
On the river, with great views of the skyline; popular for Sunday brunch. Live piano at night. Prix fixe (lunch) $42; brunch $55; entrées $120.

Frankies Spuntino (B4) 7
→ *457 Court St (4th Place and Luquer); Tel. (718) 403 0033; Daily 11am–11pm (midnight Fri-Sat)*
A garden out back and modern Italian cooking. No reservations. Entrées $10–20. Also at 570 Hudson St (W 11th St) (B4). German Alpine cuisine nearby at their Prime Meats; they also run Café Pedlar, 210 Court St (B3).

Ganso Ramen (C3) 8

OVER CLUB

STERLING PLACE

BIRD

→ *25 Bond St (Livingston) Tel. (718) 403 0900; Daily 11.30am–10pm (11pm Fri-Sat)*
An open kitchen and a daily changing menu of perfect ramen. No reservations. Ramen $15–16.

La Vara (B3) 9
→ *268 Clinton St (Verandah Pl); Tel. (718) 422 0065 Mon-Fri 5–11pm (midnight Fri); Sat-Sun 11.30am–midnight (10pm Sun)*
Delicious Spanish food drawing on Middle Eastern ingredients. Small plates from $3, large plates from $15. Their coffee shop, Tekoá, a few doors down, serves breakfast and lunch.

Convivium Osteria (C4) 10
→ *68 5th Ave (Bergen) Tel. (718) 857 1833; Mon-Fri noon–3pm, 5–11pm (11.30pm Fri); Sat-Sun 5–10pm (11.30pm Sat)*
In three romantic, rustic rooms enjoy the cooking of Italy, Spain and Portugal. Entrées $18–35.

ICE-CREAM PARLOR, CAFÉS

One Girl Cookies (B3) 11
→ *68 Dean St (Smith) Tel. (212) 675 4996 Mon-Fri 8am–7pm (8pm Fri); Sat-Sun 9am–7pm*
Great selection of decadent desserts.

Ample Hills Creamery (D4) 12
→ *623 Vanderbilt Ave (St Mark's); Tel. (347) 240 3926 Daily noon–10pm (11pm Fri)*
Delicious organic homemade ice-cream: try the salty hazelnut with chocolate covered sunflower seeds.

Mile End Deli (B3) 13
→ *97 Hoyt St (Atlantic) Tel. (718) 852 7510; Daily 8am (10am Sat–Sun)–11pm (10pm Sun-Wed)*
All ingredients are fresh and cooked on site; there is also a dinner menu.

Four & Twenty Blackbirds (B5) 14
→ *439 3rd Ave (8th) Tel. (718) 499 2917 Mon-Sat 8am (9am Sat)–8pm; Sun 10am–7pm*
A changing menu of pies to buy by the slice or whole; don't miss the salted caramel apple or lavender honey.

BARS, CONCERTS

Clover Club (B3) 15
→ *210 Smith St (Baltic) Tel. (718) 855 7939 Mon-Fri 4pm–2am (4am Fri); Sat-Sun 10.30am–4am (1am Sun)*
Old-world charm with a trendy edge: bartenders in vests, chandeliers and a crackling fireplace.

Brooklyn Inn (B3) 16
→ *148 Hoyt St (Bergen) Tel. (718) 522 2525 Daily 4pm–4am*
A former poets' hangout with an 1800s carved wood bar, stained-glass windows and a juke box.

St Ann's Warehouse (B2) 17
→ *Tobacco Warehouse, Brooklyn Bridge Park Tel. (718) 254 8779 (box office: Tue-Sat 1–7pm)*
Cutting-edge plays and performances – Wooster Group, Mabou Mines, Karen O among them.

Royal Palms (B4) 18
→ *514 Union St (Nevins and 3rd Ave); Tel. (347) 223 4410 Mon-Fri 6pm–midnight (2am Thu, Fri); Sat-Sun 2pm–midnight (2am Sat)*
This expansive 1970s Palm Beach-themed bar houses ten shuffleboard courts, rotating food trucks and great drinks.

Lavender Lake (B4) 19
→ *383 Carroll St (Bond) Tel. (347) 799 2154 Daily 4pm–midnight (1am Thu, 2am Fri-Sat)*
A converted carriage house, with inventive cocktails and a perfect menu; also a light-strung backyard.

SHOPPING

Bird (B3) 20
→ *220 Smith St (Butler) Tel. (718) 797 3774 Mon-Fri noon–8pm; Sat-Sun 11am–7pm*
Women's and men's clothing and accessories – Phillip Lim, A.P.C. and Thakoon among them.

Sterling Place (C3) 21
→ *363 Atlantic Ave (Bond) Tel. (718) 797 5667; Daily 11am (11.30am Sun)–6.30pm*
Unusual gifts, rugs, antique model ships, board games and more. Also at 148 and 352 Seventh Ave.

Diane T (B3) 22
→ *174 Court St (Bergen) Tel. (718) 923 5777; Tue-Sat 11am–7.30pm (6.30pm Sat); Sun 1–5.30pm*
Well-edited selection of women's clothes and accessories.

Consignment Brooklyn (C3) 23
→ *371 Atlantic Ave (Bond) Tel. (718) 522 3522 Daily 11am–7pm (6pm Sun)*
Vintage womenswear and accessories.

Saipua (A4) 24
→ *177 Dwight St (Van Dyke St); Tel. (718) 624 2929 Wed-Sun noon–7pm*
Flowers, hand-made soap, and other items that make the perfect gift.

NEW YORK TRANSIT MUSEUM

BROOKLYN ACADEMY OF MUSIC

BROOKLYN MUSEUM

PROSPECT PARK

BROOKLYN BOTANIC GARDEN

ıy at being guards or
vers). One platform
s every type of car used
ce 1904, complete
h old ads of the period.

**Brooklyn
useum** (D5)
*200 Eastern Parkway
(718) 638 5000; Wed-Sun
m–6pm (10pm Thu, 11pm
t Sat of each month)*
e 12 departments
lude collections
Egyptian, Asiatic,
pressionist and American
. Retrospectives of
portant contemporary
ists have included
squiat and Murakami, as
ll as Gilbert & George. In
04, the glass and metal
Rubin pavilion was built in front of the 19th-century Beaux-Arts façade as the museum's new entrance and lobby.

★ Prospect Park (D5)
→ Entrance on Grand Army Plaza; Tel. (718) 965 8951 Daily 5am–1am
Laid out in 1867 by the designers of Central Park, Olmsted and Vaux, this park (585 acres) contains the only area of natural woodland in Brooklyn. In the northwest corner is a large field where concerts are given in summer, and in the east is a leafy ravine and a zoo. To the south is a 60-acre lake, great for boating in fine weather. It is a more rustic park than its Manhattan rival, and popular among the locals for Sunday outings.

★ Brooklyn Botanic Garden (D5)
→ 900 Washington Ave Tel. (718) 623 7200 Tue-Sun 8am (Sat-Sun 10am)–6pm (10am–4.30pm Nov-Feb)
This 52-acre botanic garden in the northeast corner of Prospect Park was laid out in 1910, and contains more than 10,000 species of plants. There are gardens within the garden too: Cranford Rose Garden is a beautiful spot in early summer; the Fragrance Garden has scented plants (designed with the vision-impaired in mind); and the Shakespeare Garden has flowers and herbs mentioned in the works of the English dramatist. Look out too for the Japanese Garden, whose cherry trees flower in April during the Cherry Blossom Festival.

★ Brooklyn Academy of Music (BAM) (C3)
→ 30 Lafayette Ave Tel. (718) 636 4100
This 1908 venue hosts important theater, opera, concerts and dance. There is also the Harvey Theater and a cinematheque.

MOMA PS1

DORSKY GALLERY

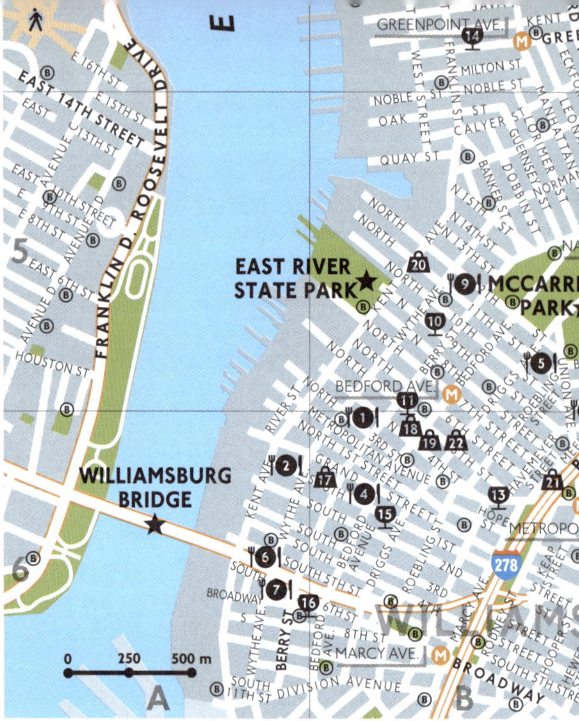

◀ Map I

★ Williamsburg Bridge (A6)
At the time of its construction (1896–1903), the all-steel Williamsburg Bridge held the record for the longest suspension bridge in the world (7,308 ft). The jazz saxophonist Sonny Rollins used to spend hours practicing on the 'Willy B' when he lived on the Lower East Side in the 1950s and 60s.

★ East River State Park (B5)
→ *90 Kent Ave (Ninth)*
Tel. (718) 782 2731
Daily 9am–dusk
Opened in 2007, the park stretches along the East River for several dozen yards. It was laid out on the site of a 19th-century dock, of which several features remain: old cobblestones, a railroad track. It offers great views of Williamsburg Bridge and midtown Manhattan skyscrapers.

★ MoMA PS1 (C3)
→ *22-25 Jackson Ave (46th)*
Tel. (718) 784 2084
Thu-Mon noon–6pm
Moved in 1976 to a former public school, this cutting-edge exhibition space became, in 2002, part of MoMA's contemporary wing. Its many exhibitions (there are more than 50 each year) have included James Turrell and Richard Serra. On Saturdays in summer it becomes the venue for outdoor concerts known as Warm up Parties (3–9pm), showcasing new musical talent.

★ Hunters Point Historic District (C3)
→ *45th Ave (21st and 23rd)*
This block of elegantly proportioned brownstone houses is a reminder of the prosperity of Queens in the 19th century. The relocation of the Long Island City Railroad terminus and the nearby waterway made the area an important urban junction in the 1860s. In the following decade, developers Spencer Root and John Rust built these houses, which were abandoned by their well-to-do inhabitants when the noisy overhead railway arrived in 1909. There are all kinds of sty to be seen in the houses including Italianate, Queen Anne and French Second Empire.

★ Dorsky Gallery (C3)
→ *11-03 45th Ave (11th)*
Tel. (718) 937 6317
Thu-Mon 11am–6pm
This not-for-profit art spa shows independently

WILLIAMSBURG BRIDGE

EAST RIVER STATE PARK

MCCARREN PARK

▲ Map C/E

Many young artists and writers have flocked to the north of Brooklyn, Williamsburg. Bedford Avenue is at the heart of this area, a street filled with lively bars and colorful boutiques. Queens, to the north, is conveniently only 15 minutes from Grand Central Station. Long Island City (LIC) is a fascinating labyrinth of avant-garde museums and artists' studios. A few stations along is Astoria, a multicultural quarter popular with the Greek and Brazilian communities.

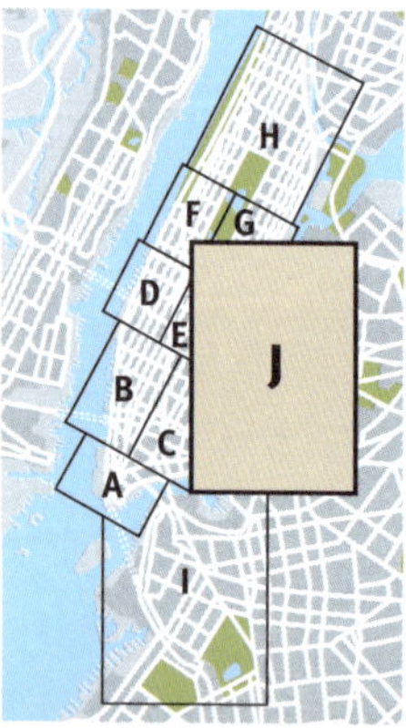

MAISON PREMIERE

MISS FAVELA

RESTAURANTS

Egg (B6) 1
→ *109 N 3rd St (Berry)*
Tel. (718) 302 5151; Daily 7am (8am Sat-Sun)–5pm
Phenomenal sandwiches with Southern roots (pulled pork) and fried chicken, organic produce, salads and breakfasts too. Sandwiches $9–19.

Cafe de La Esquina (A6) 2
→ *225 Wythe Ave*
Tel. (718) 393 5500 Tue-Fri noon–10pm (11pm Wed-Thu, midnight Fri); Sat-Sun 11am–midnight (10pm Sun)
An outpost of its NoLIta sister, a cantina in a colorful 50s-style diner with a breezy, take-out taqueria and a pleasant patio. Entrées $5–13 (taqueria); $10–22 (diner).

Roberta's (off D6) 3
→ *261 Moore St (Bogart)*
Tel. (718) 417 1118
Daily 11am (10am Sat-Sun)–midnight
Great artisanal pizza, along with salumi with duck prosciutto. Pizza $11–18. No reservations.

Maison Premiere (B6) 4
→ *298 Bedford Ave*
Tel. (347) 335 0446
Mon-Fri 4pm–2am (4am Thu-Fri); Sat 11am–4am; Sun 11am–2am
Evoking the Belle Époque – a horse-shoe shaped bar, small tables inside or in the garden under an arbor. Try up to 30 kinds of oysters, *crudo*, vegetable soup or venison tartare. Reserve for parties of 6 or more. Entrées $21–31.

Lilia (B5) 5
→ *567 Union Ave (North 10th); Tel. (718) 576 3095*
Daily 5.30–11pm
In a room of white furniture and bleached wood, try Missy Robbins' ethereal pappardelle with veal bolognese or the black bass in a salsa verde. Reserve. Entrées $20–30.

Miss Favela (A6) 6
→ *57 S Fifth St (Wythe)*
Tel. (718) 230 4040
Daily noon–midnight (1am Fri-Sat)
Brazilian specialties such as *feijoada* (stewed beef and pork with beans) and *moqueca* (fish stew). At night, be prepared to dance the samba. Entrées $17–29; cash only.

Marlow & Sons (A6) 7
→ *81 Broadway (Berry)*
Tel. (718) 384 1441
Daily 8am–midnight
For breakfast, lunch, dinner: menus change

UE BOTTLE COFFEE

KNITTING FACTORY

CATBIRD

daily but in winter you may find duck liver pâté, rabbit leg, trout. They own 'Diner' next door. Reservations for parties of 6 or more. Entrées $26–28.

Llama Inn (B5) 8
→ *50 Withers St (Meeker Ave); Tel. (718) 387 3434 Mon-Fri 5–10pm (1am Thu-Fri); Sat-Sun 11am–3pm, 5pm–1am (10pm Sun)*
In a bright airy space, an open kitchen and delicious Peruvian/ American dishes: duck sausage, or tuna *tiraditu* with ponzu, lime, cucumber and avocado. Entrées $16–19.

Leuca (B5) 9
→ *William Vale Hotel, 111 N 12th St (Wythe Ave); Tel. (718) 581 5900; Daily 7am–3pm (4pm Sat-Sun), 5.30–11pm (midnight Sat-Sun)*
In an airy space with a tiled floor and leather seating, Andrew Carmellini's nod to Abruzzo and Sicily: pastas, wood-fired pizzas, fish and meats. Entrees $17–44.

ICE-CREAM PARLOR, CAFÉ, PATISSERIE

Van Leeuwen Artisan Ice Cream (B5) 10
→ *204 Wythe Ave; Tel. (929) 337 6907; Daily 7am (9am Sat-Sun)–midnight*
Artisanal classic and vegan ice cream and house-made pastries in a sleek, bright space; bold flavors like Candied Ginger, Earl Grey Tea and Sicilian Pistachio.

Blue Bottle Coffee (B6) 11
→ *160 Berry St (Fifth and Sixth); Tel. (718) 387 4160 Daily 7am–7pm*
Beans are roasted on site; delicious homemade *biscotti*, pastries and sandwiches.

Patisserie Tomoko (C5) 12
→ *568 Union Ave (Richardson and Frost) Tel. (718) 388 7121 Tue-Sun noon–9pm (11pm Fri-Sat, 8pm Sun)*
Exquisite French-Japanese pastries, and wine or sake. Tomoko trained at Le Bernardin.

BARS, CONCERTS

Knitting Factory (B6) 13
→ *361 Metropolitan Ave (Havemeyer) Tel. (347) 529 6696 Bar: daily 6pm–3.30am*
This post-rock bar and concert hall has a bold program of experimental and underground music; reasonable prices.

Ramona (B4) 14
→ *113 Franklin St (Kent) Tel. (347) 227 8164; Daily 5pm (1pm Sat-Sun)–4am*
Expertly crafted cocktails and vintage décor draws a vibrant crowd to this upscale two-level bar.

Bar Omar (B6) 15
→ *188 Grand St (Bedford and Driggs); Tel. (718) 388 0411; Tue-Fri 4pm–midnight (1am Fri); Sat-Sun 11am–1am*
Offshoot of Chez Omar in Paris, this lively Algerian spot offers mouthwatering couscous and tagines. Reservations for parties of 6 or more.

Loosie Rouge (A6) 16
→ *91 S Sixth St (Berry) Mon-Fri 6pm–2am; Sat-Sun noon–4pm, 6pm–2am*
Draft cocktails in a cool but cozy bar – an upright piano for a New Orleans vibe. For oysters Bloomberg and po'boys, head next door to Loosie's Kitchen.

SHOPPING

Antoinette (B6) 17
→ *119 Grand St (Berry) Tel. (718) 387 8664; Tue-Sun noon–7pm (6pm Sun)*
Well-curated vintage and modern clothing for men and women in an attractive space.

Swords-Smith (B6) 18
→ *98 S Fourth St (Berry) Tel. (347) 599 2969 Daily noon (11am Sat)–8pm (7pm Sun)*
Carefully edited women's clothing by up-and-coming designers.

Spoonbill & Sugartown (B6) 19
→ *218 Bedford Ave (Fifth) Tel. (718) 387 7322 Daily 10am–10pm*
A bookstore specializing in art, architecture and design.

Williamsburg Flea Market (B5) 20
→ *50 Kent Ave (N 11th) May-Dec: Sun 10am–5pm*
By the East River, vintage clothing, trinkets and gourmet food stands.

10 Ft. Single by Stella Dallas (B6) 21
→ *185 N Sixth St (Metropolitan); Tel. (718) 486 9482; Daily 12.30–7.30pm (8pm Sat-Sun)*
A vintage shop with clothes for men and women: button-down shirts in 70s prints, summer dresses, boots and shoes.

Catbird (B6) 22
→ *219 Bedford Ave (N 5th St) Tel. 718 599 3457 Daily noon–8pm (6pm Sun)*
Jewelry, accessories and unique gifts.

HUNTERS POINT HISTORIC DISTRICT

FISHER LANDAU CENTER FOR ART

MUSEUM OF THE MOVING IMAGE

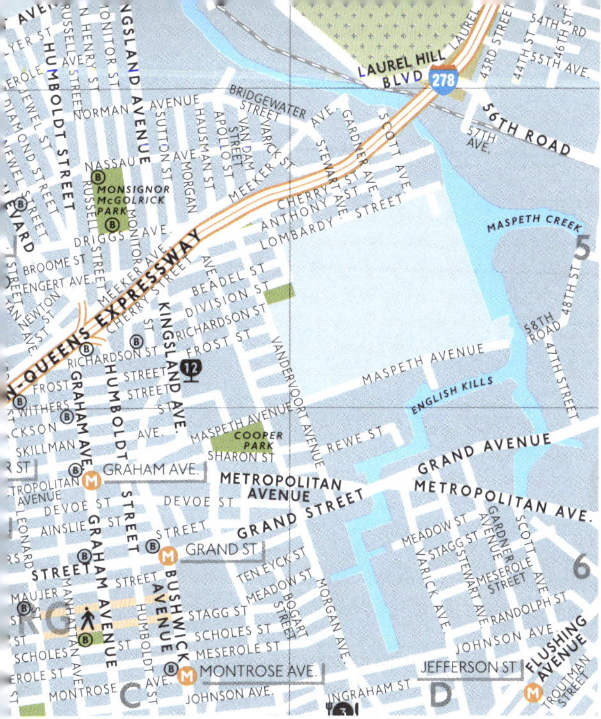

NOGUCHI MUSEUM

SOCRATES SCULPTURE PARK

rated exhibitions of
ntemporary art, from
ra Maar to R. Cumming.

**Noguchi
useum** (C1)
*9-01 33rd Rd (Vernon and
1th); Tel. (212) 204 7088
d-Fri 10am–5pm; Sat-Sun
m–6pm*
small museum devoted
the Japanese sculptor
mu Noguchi (1904–88),
signed by the artist. The
rden and ground floor
leries house the
rmanent collection;
stairs are temporary
nibitions. The shop has
mes furniture, objects
d Noguchi's famous
e-paper light sculptures.

★ Museum of the Moving Image (D2)
→ *36 01 35th Ave (37th)
Tel. (718) 777 6888
Wed-Fri 10.30am–2pm (8pm first Fri of the month between May-Sep); Sat 11am–6pm; Sun 11am–7pm*
The museum, devoted to the audiovisual arts, is located next to the Kaufman-Astoria Studios, and gives a behind-the-scenes glimpse of movies and television through interactive installations.

★ Socrates Sculpture Park (C1)
→ *Broadway / Vernon Blvd
Tel. (718) 956 1819
Daily 10am–sunset*
This open-air sculpture museum is set in a park opposite Roosevelt Island; also screens movies and hosts cultural events.

★ Fisher Landau Center for Art (D2)
→ *38-27 30th St (38th)
Tel. (718) 937 0727
Thu-Mon noon–5pm*
This former parachute factory was converted in 1991 by British architect Max Gordon to house the Emily Fisher Landau Foundation, amassed since 1960. It contains 1,500 works by such artists as Jasper Johns, Andy Warhol, Matthew Barney and Cy Twombly.

★ Franklin D. Roosevelt Four Freedoms Park (B2-3)
→ *East Road, Roosevelt Island; Tel. (212) 204 8831
Wed-Mon 9am–7pm*
Take the tramway at 59th and 2nd to this beautiful park designed by Louis I. Kahn, with a bust of FDR by Jo Davidson, a 'granite' room, monumental stairs, *allées* of linden trees and lawns.

★ McCarren Park (B5)
A pool here turns into an ice-skating rink in winter, but its outdoor Northside music festival and SummerScreen series are the big draw.

Best of the best

Ten must-have experiences to seek out in New York

Photograph Manhattan
Join a long line of renowned photographers and take your camera onto the streets of New York to capture fleeting moments, architectural details and striking design. For urban landscapes, head to Williamsburg Bridge (**J** A6) or cross Brooklyn Bridge and station yourself in Brooklyn Bridge Park (**I** B2).

Take in a show (D D1-3)
Musicals, from *Les Misérables, The Book of Mormon* and *The Lion King* to *The Phantom of the Opera* and *Spamalot* have brought pleasure to tourists and New Yorkers alike. Take in a Broadway or off-Broadway show (for something edgier). Around Times Square the illuminated billboards are shows in their own right.
→ *Discount tickets at the TKTS kiosk on Times Square* (**D** E3)*; daily 3pm (2pm Tue) –8pm (7pm Sun) for evening shows*

Shop in SoHo and NoLIta (B-C)
Walk the streets of SoHo – south of Houston and north of Canal – now a clothes-shopping mecca, from high-end Prada and Chanel to Uniqlo and TopShop, as well as books at McNally Jackson (*52 Prince St,* **C** A5). Just east, also south of Houston, is NoLIta, with a more village-like feel, smaller streets and boutiques on Elizabeth, Mott and Mulberry Sts.

Browse art in Chelsea or the Lower East Side
On a week day or a Saturday, join art mavens browsing shows in the more than 350 galleries in the blocks from 18th to 29th between Tenth and the highway or Eleventh avenues. Or check out the 75 galleries below East Houston.
→ *For a bite to eat during your Chelsea excursion, try Bottino (Tenth Ave/24th and 25th), The Red Cat (Tenth Ave/23rd and 24th), Cookshop (see* **B**)*, Lucien (First Ave at First) and Cherche Midi (corner of Houston and Bowery)*

Go to Brooklyn (I)
Visit the tree-lined streets of Boerum Hill, Cobble Hill and Carroll Gardens. In Cobble Hill, on Henry Street, there is Lucali restaurant and shops such as Bird or Diane T; and don't forget the Brooklyn Museum or the galleries along Front Street in DUMBO.

Walk the High Line
You can get onto this former train track (**B** A3), planted like a garden two stories above the street, at Gansevoort and Washington streets

BROOKLYN BRIDGE

and walk up to 34th Street. Then cross the West Side Highway to the landscaped walkway along the Hudson and head down to Battery Park. Don't miss a walk on the East River Esplanade (**C** D4-5), with green spaces around the Battery Maritime Building and piers 15 and 35 – part of a 2-mile-long public area on the East River.

Take to the water

Being on the water off Manhattan is thrilling at sunset. In fine weather, ride the giant speedboat, *The Beast* (no toddlers allowed) for half an hour in the harbor. Or cruise the more sedate Circle Line around Manhattan.

→ *Cruises leave from Pier 83 (W 42nd) and 12th Ave; circleline42.com*

Indulge in a cocktail with a view

Once there was only the Piano Bar of the Rainbow Room on the 65th floor of Rockefeller Center (**D** E2); now there are rooftop bars, both inside and outside. Downtown is Le Bain on the 18th floor of The Standard (**B** A3) or Mr Purple on the 15th floor of the Hotel Indigo (*171 Ludlow St*, **C** B4). Midtown there is the dramatic Plunge Bar + Lounge with a pool on the 15th floor of the Gansevoort Park Avenue (*420 Park Ave South at 29th*, **E** B6). If you are on Fifth Avenue at 55th Street, lounge at Salon de Ning (**E** A1). Near the Hudson is Ink48 (*653 11th Ave at 48th*, **D** B2), the hotel with David Rockwell's reflecting pool and bar on the 16th floor. The pool at the Viceroy (*124 W 57th St*) is on the 29th floor. On the Upper West Side, a deck on the 12th floor of The Empire Hotel (*44 W 63rd St*, **G** A4) overlooks Lincoln Center. On the Upper East Side, visit the Metropolitan Museum (**G** C1) and try the Garden Café on the roof, overlooking Central Park.

Listen to jazz

In Harlem at the Apollo Theater (**H** B3), Minton's (*206 W 118th St*, **H** C3) and clubs like Smoke Jazz & Supper Club (**H** A5); or in midtown to Jazz at Lincoln Center in the Rose Theater (**F** C6), Dizzy's Club Coca Cola (**F** C6) or Birdland (*315 W 44th St at Eighth*, **D** D3). Downtown, in the Village, there is the Blue Note (**B** C4), Village Vanguard (**B** B3) and Smalls Jazz Club (*183 W Tenth St at Seventh*, **B** C3).

Delight in Asian food

New York's Asian communities are steeped in sophisticated culinary traditions. The aroma of Beijing duck hangs in the air in Chinatown, while elsewhere there is an abundance of Malaysian, Japanese, Korean, Indian, Cambodian, etc. stores and restaurants.

→ *Momofuku Noodle Bar* (**C** B3), *Hangawi* (**E** A6), *Pongal* (**E** B6)

TIMES SQUARE

... and even on Sundays

Brunch

→ *Generally $10–30*

A New York institution. **Augustine (A** D2), **Prune (C** B4), **Buttermilk Channel (I** A5).

Museums

Of a very high standard; can be crowded.

Parks

Something for everyone: watch street performers, see open-air concerts, enjoy a hot dog or ice cream...or simply lounge around on the grass. **Central Park (G** B2), **Prospect Park (I** D5).

Flea markets

Aside from the big names, there is a wealth of small impromptu markets: behind a church, on an empty lot, in a park...

Shopping

→ *Generally 10am–7pm*

Stores stay open in SoHo (**B**), Midtown (**E**), DUMBO (**I**) and Williamsburg (**J**).

Shows

The city that never sleeps has jazz clubs, concert halls and theaters that are as busy as ever. **Village Vanguard (B** B3), **The Iridium (D** D2), **The Beacon Theatre (F** B3), **Hammerstein Ballroom** (*311 W 34th St*, **D** D4), **Playstation Theater** (*1515 Broadway*, **D** E3), **Gramercy Theater** (*127 E 23rd St*, **C** A1).

Day trips

LONG BEACH

THE CLOISTERS

Excursions within 1–2 hours of the city... plus good places to eat

Tarrytown and Sleepy Hollow
→ *Metro North train from Grand Central Station to Tarrytown (45 mins)*
Historic towns on the Hudson River: Sleepy Hollow is the birthplace of Washington Irving, author of *The Legend of Sleepy Hollow*. In Tarrytown are the hiking trails of Pocantico Hills, where you can also tour Kykuit, the Rockefeller family estate, an underground art gallery with a collection of Picasso tapestries, and the Coach Barn, with its collection of classic cars and carriages. For lunch or dinner try **RiverMarket Bar and Kitchen** (*127 W Main St, Tarrytown*).

Flushing Meadows – Corona Park
→ *Subway to Mets-Willets Point (line 7), approx 30 mins*
Queens Museum: *New York City Building; Tel. (718) 592 9700; Wed-Sun 11am–5pm*
New York Hall of Science: *47-01 111th St/47th Ave Tel. (718) 699 0005 Mon-Fri 9.30am–5pm; Sat-Sun 10am–6pm*
The vast site of the 1939 Universal Exhibition, housing the Queens Museum (with an extraordinary model of the city), the New York Hall of Science (interactive exhibits, including two NASA rocket heads) and a zoo. The park also plays host to the US Open.

Park Side Restaurant
→ *107-1 Corona Ave Tel. (718) 271 9274 Mon-Sat noon–11.30pm; Sun 12.30–10pm*
An Italian restaurant specializing in seafood and grilled meat. Entrées $16–40.

The Cloisters
→ *Fort Tryon Park; subway to 190th St (line A), approx 45 mins; Tel. (212) 923 3700 Daily 10am–5.15pm (4.45pm in winter)*
Whole sections of medieval churches, chapels and cloisters imported from Europe and reconstituted here between 1934 and 1938 (see the seven Unicorn Tapestries); overlooks unspoiled banks of the Hudson River.

New Leaf Café
→ *1 Margaret Corbin Drive, Fort Tryon Park; Tel. (212) 568 5323; Mon-Fri noon–7pm (9pm Fri); Sat-Sun 11am–3.30pm, 4–9pm (8pm Sun)*
A charming stone cottage serving mostly local organic food (salad, cheese from Vermont). Large terrace in summer. Entrées $16–28.

Bronx Park
→ ***New York Botanical Garden:*** *2900 Southern Blvd; subway to Bedford Park Blvd (lines B, D, 4), approx 50 mins; Tel. (718) 817 8700 Tue-Sun 10am–6pm;* ***Bronx Zoo:*** *Bronx River Parkway; subway to Pelham Parkway (lines 2, 5); Tel. (718) 367 1010; Daily 10am–5pm (4.30pm in winter)*
A beautiful park dissected by the Bronx River, its banks lined with maple trees. Two major attractions: one of the world's biggest botanical gardens, with over 50 themed areas and an

CONEY ISLAND

EXCURSION SITES

imposing early-20th-c. greenhouse; and the zoo, home to more than 4,000 animals and 650 species.

Pine Tree Café
→ *2900 Southern Blvd*
Opening hours as gardens
In the heart of the botanical garden, an informal café with an extensive terrace. Salads, freshly made sandwiches and pizzas from a log-fired oven. Entrées $11–34.

Coney Island
→ *Subway to Coney Island (lines D, F, Q), approx 1 hr*
Fairly deserted during the week but comes alive at the weekend. See the famous Luna Park funfair and the famous 3-mile boardwalk linking Coney Island with Brighton Beach (also known as Little Odessa). Ukranian and Russian Jews settled here in the 1970s, hence the store and restaurant signs written in the Cyrillic alphabet.

Skovorodka
→ *615 Brighton Beach Ave*
Tel. (718) 615 3096
Daily 11am–10pm (11pm Sat)
A taste of Russia: eggplant caviar, Borscht, blinis and a fine selection of vodkas. Live music at the weekend. Entrées $10–24.

Long Beach
→ *LIRR train from Penn Station; approx 1 hr*
In summer, the white sandy beaches lining this long, thin island provide a refreshing escape from the stifling heat of the city.

Atlantica
→ *Allegria Hotel, 80 W Broadway, Long Beach*
Tel. (516) 992 3730; Mon-Fri 6.30am–10pm; Sat-Sun 6.30am–10pm, 5–10pm
Fresh fish and seafood by the edge of the ocean. Entrées $10–37.

Dia: Beacon
→ *Metro North train from Grand Central Station to Beekman St, approx 1½ hrs*
Tel. (845) 440 0100; Jan-Mar: Fri-Mon 11am–4pm; April-Dec: Thu-Mon 11am–6pm (4pm Nov-Dec); mta.info
A former Nabisco box-printing factory plays host to works by Joseph Beuys, Louise Bourgeois, Dan Flavin, Sol LeWitt and Andy Warhol. Don't miss *North, East, South, West* (1967), the gigantic 'negative' sculptures hollowed out of the ground by Michael Heizer, or Richard Serra's dizzying *Ellipses* (2000).

Café du Dia: Beacon
→ *Same opening hours as the museum (from 10.30am)*
Salads, quiches, burgers and sandwiches. Entrées $6–12.

Storm King Art Center
→ *Old Pleasant Hill Road, Mountainville, Cornwall*
Coach USA (Short Line Bus) from Port Authority Bus Terminal, 8.30am and 10am, approx 1½ hrs; Tel. (845) 534 3115; Wed-Sun 10am–4.30pm/5.30pm/8pm depending on season; see coachusa.com
This sculpture park of more than 500 acres, has large-scale pieces and land art. See Maya Lin's *Wave Field*, Andy Galsworthy's 750-ft-long dry stone wall, and works by Mark di Suvero, Alexander Calder and Richard Serra, set amidst magnificent landscape.

Storm King Café
→ *April-Nov: Wed-Sun 11am–3.30pm*
Local, organic produce in this café inside the park. Entrées $6–10.

Transportation in Manhattan

Manhattan Subway Map
September 2015
Plan Ahead Online
Use Trip Planner+
at www.mta.info
for subway & bus directions
LEGEND
Terminal
Station Name
4·5·6
Full-time Service
Part-time Service
Local Service only
All trains stop (local and express service)
Free subway transfer
Free out-of-system subway transfer (excluding single-ride ticket)
Rush hour line extension
BROOKLYN
EAST RIVER
42 St-Port Authority Bus Terminal A·C·E
Grand Central 42 St·S·4·5·6·7
14 St-Union Sq L·N·Q·R·4·5·6
Delancey St-Essex St F·J·M·Z
World Trade Center·E
Brooklyn Bridge-City Hall·4·5·6
South Ferry·1
Whitehall St South Ferry·R
Bowling Green·4·5
©2015 Metropolitan Transportation Authority. Unauthorized duplication prohibited.

Manhattan Bus Map
September 2015
Plan Ahead Online
Use Trip Planner+
at www.mta.info
for subway & bus directions
LEGEND
Full-time Service (Every day 7 a.m.-10 p.m.)
Part-time Service
Select Bus Service bus stop. Fare is paid before boarding.
Direction of Service (two-way service has no arrows)
Full-time Terminal
Part-time Terminal
34 +selectbusservice
34A +selectbusservice
15 +selectbusservice
M15 Local
BROOKLYN
EAST RIVER
MANHATTAN BRIDGE
BROOKLYN BRIDGE
©2015 Metropolitan Transportation Authority. Unauthorized duplication prohibited.

Index

Entries are followed by a letter in bold (**A, B, C...**) which refers to the corresponding area and map. Those followed by a ★ are sights featured on the pages with maps. The symbol ✪ refers to the Top Ten sights page at the front of the guide.

EATING OUT

SHOPPING